understands Jesus Christ to be the completion and fulfillment of every major Old Testament tradition history. This means, says the author, that neither Jesus Christ nor the church can be understood apart from the Old Testament, and any preacher who wishes to proclaim the New Testament gospel must of necessity also proclaim the Old Testament's message.

The final section of the book is devoted to the practical task of demonstrating how to preach from the Old Testament. The author discusses what passages to use from the Old Testament, and texts are suggested for the entire church year. She then shows, by sermon outlines and illustrations, how not to use the texts. The author also presents valid methods of preaching from the Old Testament, and these are concretely illustrated by sermons which she has preached in various congregations.

ELIZABETH ACHTEMEIER is Visiting Professor in the Homiletics Department, Union Theological Seminary, Richmond, Virginia. She was formerly Adjunct Professor of Old Testament, Lancaster Theological Seminary. She is a graduate of Stanford University, Union Theological Seminary, and Columbia University (Ph.D.), and took postgraduate work at the Universities of Heidelberg and Basel.

THE OLD TESTAMENT
AND THE PROCLAMATION
OF THE GOSPEL

THE OLD TESTAMENT
AND THE
PROCLAMATION
OF THE GOSPEL

by
ELIZABETH ACHTEMEIER

THE WESTMINSTER PRESS
Philadelphia

Unless otherwise stated, all Scripture quotations are from the Revised Standard Version of the Bible, copyright, 1946 and 1952, by the Division of Christian Education of the National Council of Churches, and used by permission.

Book design by Dorothy Alden Smith

Published by The Westminster Press ⑱
Philadelphia, Pennsylvania

PRINTED IN THE UNITED STATES OF AMERICA

Library of Congress Cataloging in Publication Data

Achtemeier, Elizabeth Rice.
    The Old Testament and the proclamation of the Gospel.

    1. Bible. O.T.—Criticism, interpretation, etc.
2. Bible. N.T.—Relation to O.T. 3. Bible. O.T.—
Homiletical use. I. Title.
BS1171.2.A25   221.6′6   73–7863
ISBN 0–664–20974–2

To Bud

with whom
Ephesians 5:31–32
has become reality

Contents

Part Three
PREACHING FROM THE OLD TESTAMENT

Part One

THE PRESENT DILEMMA
OF THE CHURCH

CHAPTER I

The Loss of the Bible
in the Church

THE MAINSTREAM of American Protestantism now faces a crisis situation of major proportions. It is in danger of losing all its Biblical foundations.

It is now possible in this country to carry on the expected work of a Protestant congregation with no reference to the Bible whatsoever. The worship services of the church can be divorced from Biblical models and become the celebration of the congregation's life together and of its more or less vaguely held common beliefs in some god. Folk songs, expressive of American culture, can replace the psalms of the church. Art forms and aesthetic experiences can be used as substitutes for communion with God. The preacher's opinions or ethical views can be made replacements for the word from the Biblical text. The Sacraments can be turned into expressions of simply the congregation's fellowship together. But the amazing thing is that no one in the pew on Sunday morning may notice. Indeed, such a worship service may win praise from some quarters as "contemporary" and "relevant."

In the realm of the pastoral ministry of the church, it is now not unusual to find that distinctively Christian counseling and the "cure of souls" has been replaced by totally secularized insights and exercises from modern psychology and group therapy. Sensitivity training and encounter groups can be conducted with no Biblical reference whatsoever, and the definition of what is "normal" and "good" is usually taken from the surrounding culture.

As a substitute for Christian education and training in the Biblical heritage and belief and practice, many church schools now concentrate, in both youth and adult groups, on the social, political, and ethical issues of the day, bringing to the discussion of such issues norms derived solely from current liberalism. It is not unusual to find that what is passed down in the Sunday school to the next generation is simply the most widely held secular moral and social values of present-day society.

As for the church's mission, some of the congregations most active "in the world" have entirely left behind any attention to the ethical demands of the gospel and are now pursuing social action programs prompted only by the crises of their communities or more often by the ideals and visions of national denominational boards and leaders.

To be sure, it is rare to find all these phenomena in one local church, and most congregations at least pay lip service to the Biblical heritage in their worship practices and Christian education. There is usually one Bible study group still operative in most churches, although it may involve only the older women of the congregation. Most Sunday schools still have some part of their curriculum devoted to the Bible, although it is noteworthy that children usually study about the Bible from a textbook rather than from the Bible itself. Almost every pastor still reads from the New Testament from the lectern on Sunday morning, although there are exceptions to even this generalization.

Nevertheless, there can be no doubt that the Scriptures are losing ground in the larger denominations of American Protestantism, and the attention and the authority granted to the Bible by most congregations are now superficial at best. Certainly there is a growing and almost universal ignorance of the Bible on the part of the church's lay people. And now there is a mounting frustration among the clergy over using Biblical texts in preaching. To borrow James Smart's phrase, there is today a "strange silence of the Bible in the church." [1]

This is not a situation to be taken lightly, for unless the church's life is rooted and nourished in the Bible, it has no possibility of being Christian.

In contrast to many of the ethical and social societies masquerading as Christian congregations today, the Christian church is a community which acknowledges Jesus Christ as its Lord, which knows that it is called into being and made one and sustained by his presence in its midst, and which therefore worships him as present Lord in its services and acts in the world according to his commands.

But through what other medium is Jesus Christ revealed as present Lord than through the witness of the Scriptures? His Lordship certainly is not seen in the activities of the society around us, nor does it emerge as the necessary conclusion of group discussions and sensitivity sessions. It is revealed only through that story which is given us in the Old and New Testaments. The Old Testament story looks forward to Jesus Christ; the New Testament remembers him. Without that story the Christian church has no possibility of existence.

If Jesus Christ is, as the Christian church confesses, the revelation of who God really is in this world, then any attempts to talk about God apart from the Scriptures will produce negative and idolatrous results. The God and Father of our Lord Jesus Christ *is* the God of the Bible. If the church desires to proclaim and worship and serve *that* God, then it must find him through the Bible. There is no other medium through which his fullness is revealed to us.

The fact that the Bible is being lost in the church is therefore a crisis of the most serious proportions. We are in danger of losing all relationship to the only God there is, which means, of course, that we are in danger of chaos and finally, total death.

Our society at large has proceeded for some time with no reference to God of course, and there is no doubt that ours is now a thoroughly secular nation. We assume that nature and history proceed in an unbroken chain of cause and effect, that that which is real is the visible and tangible, and that any influences which change the course of history and nature spring out of human freedom alone. In short, any transcendent activity or influence on the course of our world has been eliminated from the American world view. While church services may be held in the White House, and prayers for peace abound, few persons seriously believe that God has any effect on international relations with Russia or China. Nor does the average American feel that God affects his health and well-being, much less holds him responsible and acts toward him according to what he does to his neighbor.

The church was traditionally the witness to the activity of God within our world, but the majority of American church members have become as secularized as the society around them. They may yet hold to a pious belief in God's guidance and strengthening of them as individuals. They rarely feel that God has any relation to the events reported in their daily newspapers. As one member of our local congregation put it, "I believe in God, but I don't think he does anything." Clearly, the Biblical Lord, who acts in nature and history, has been eliminated from the scene. Judging by the attitudes of students entering seminary training, such elimination has rapidly accelerated since the beginning of the '70s.

This growing secularization of the American church is especially surprising in view of the fact that we have emerged only in the last few years from what Brevard Childs has called the Biblical Theology Movement.[2] From roughly 1940 to 1960, the American church, in concert with the churches of western Europe, experienced an overwhelming renewal—at least among its leaders!—of interest in Biblical theology. Initiated by the theologies of giants such as Barth, Brunner, and Niebuhr, propagated by the writing of Eichrodt and von Rad and Cullmann, given American form in books by G. Ernest Wright and Paul S. Minear, and taught by master teachers such as James Muilenburg, interest in the witness of the Bible to "the mighty acts of God" seemingly swept everything in the American church before it. Several Sunday school curricula were revised in the light of the new understanding, Biblical theology courses were added to the list in dozens of seminary catalogs, religious bookstores were flooded with new volumes on the meaning of Scripture. The central theme of the entire movement was that the God of the Bible acts in history and is revealed by his acts. New graduates went forth confidently from the seminaries to proclaim such facts from their pulpits. It seemed to those who experienced the Movement that the real value of the Bible had finally been uncovered, and none imagined that ensuing years would call the Movement into question. Nor did the participants in the Movement fully realize how little it actually had influenced American faith and practice.

The Biblical Theology Movement took place largely among the theologians and clergy of the church. Furthermore, its Achilles' heel was its failure to define the relation of the "history" through which God was revealed to present-day faith. By the term "history," most Biblical scholars meant the history recorded in the Bible. And it was readily acknowledged by most that that was a confessional history. But since Biblical history was confessional in nature, its relation to present history was never made clear.[3] In the Bible, God's Lordship was revealed by his action, for example, in the exodus. But to what experience of modern man could such an event possibly be compared? Did we know a God who acted in such a manner in the twentieth century, or could God be said to act in our history in any comparable way? Could modern man put any credence in such a God? If not, was our faith then built solely upon the past? Or was the Biblical witness to God's action in history solely a product of Israel's primitive world view, and did we not need after all a completely new understanding of God to fit our scientific world view? Did the Bible's confessional history finally bear no authoritative revelation for our life in the atomic age?

The Babel of confusion that arose out of the attempts to answer these questions brought forth three notable responses in the church. First, there was the attempt to redefine the nature of God and his relationship to his world. In the writings

17

of Paul Tillich and Bishop John A. T. Robinson, e.g., the transcendent God of the Bible was replaced with the Ground of Being, an immanent deity confined within the realities of this world. Faith then became an awareness of the depths of our existence. Secondly, a few radical theologians who could find no evidence of the "God who acts" in the world around them declared "God is dead" and focused their sole attention on the person of Jesus. Finally, many clergymen, laboring under the guilty burden of the failure of the church to implement the gospel in the world and finding no clear presentation of the relation of the transcendent God of the Bible to the world of the twentieth century, also turned their attention solely to Jesus as "the man for others." Out of this exclusive attention to the ethical dimensions of the gospel, there gradually developed the conviction that if God was active at all in this world, then his activity consisted not in his special mighty acts or even in his presence within his church, but rather in his participation in the struggles of those subject to the evils of racism and poverty and war. Indeed, not a few clergymen seemed to feel that their personal participation in such struggles would inject God's presence into the world. There therefore went forth from these clergy to their churches the call to service in the world as the *sole* means of relating God to life in the '60s and '70s. There alone, claimed the most radical social actionists— in the struggles for civil rights and welfare and peace—could God's active presence in our history be clearly discerned and served. Preaching was no longer important, and God was no longer to be found through his revelation of himself through Word or church. He had immersed himself in the revolutionary conflicts of the downtrodden in the world, and only by participation in such conflicts could he therefore be known and served.

Common to all three responses was the abandonment of the Bible as the authoritative medium of revealing God, and many of those who had earlier embraced the Biblical Theology Movement with great enthusiasm now turned away from the canonical authority of the Scriptures altogether.

18

Moreover, there have now developed in the United States a large number of new attempts to relate to the divine through other media. Some in the church have turned to the mystic arts of the Eastern religions as avenues of revelation. Both within and without the established church is to be found a burgeoning interest in the intricacies of astrology and the signs of the zodiac. Among the young, the use of drugs has sometimes been touted as a new means of revealing ultimate reality. Indeed, wherever one looks, one finds an enormous yearning for a communion with the divine which will issue in the healing of man's broken community: in the attempts at new life-styles in various communes and withdrawn retreats; in submission to the authority of sensitivity groups and to their "trainers"; in the total commitment of some to causes, revolutions, and movements. The hunger for God, for authority, for healing, for salvation has never been greater, it seems. But the Biblical witness is not being used, even in much of the church, to feed the sheep—at least not in the mainstream of American Protestantism.

If our Protestant churches are to recover their Biblical heritage and return to the task of proclaiming the Lordship of Jesus Christ, revealed through the Scriptures, several steps are needed.

First, the average pastor and layman must become aware of the fact that the Bible has truly been lost in the church and that modern worship, educational, psychological, and homiletical techniques are not adequate substitutes for the Bible's distinctive witness. The church should use every modern technique at its disposal to communicate the Biblical word, but at the same time, the church should realize that the technique is only a tool for proclaiming the word and not an adequate substitute for it. Otherwise the church falls into the abysmal situation of proclaiming the content of the culture out of which its tools are developed, rather than proclaiming the life-giving content of the Word of God to a culture dying for want of it.

Second, the average pastor and layman must be made aware of *how* we lost the Bible in the church. It was not the short-

19

comings of the Biblical Theology Movement nor the secularization of our society by modern science and technology which pushed the Biblical revelation out the church door. A good case can be made for the fact that the Biblical Theology Movement never really "took" in this country, among the general lay membership of the church as a whole. Childs himself has pointed out that the Movement never resulted in basic changes in Biblical commentaries, in educational policies of the church, or in ethics.[4] Rather, American Protestantism as a whole proceeded on the basis of that Biblical scholarship which grew out of Wellhausian developmentalism and which held principal sway in the church during the first three decades of the twentieth century. The effects of such scholarship are still very much with us and have determined in large measure the attitude of the nonfundamentalist wings of America's churches toward the Bible.

Third, the real and lasting contributions of the Biblical Theology Movement, isolated though they were in American church life, must be preserved for our pastors and lay people through the formulation of adequate principles for the interpretation of the Bible. The God of the Bible is indeed the God who reveals himself primarily through a history. It must be made clear, then, what the nature of that history is, what relationship that history has to our present life as Christians, and why we are able to appropriate that ancient history as our own, as the Word of God spoken to us. In short, we need some sound presuppositional bases for our hermeneutics.

Fourth, there must finally be formulated valid methodologies by which the Biblical witness to God can be proclaimed and communicated to our people through the preaching and teaching of the church. The average pastor who sits down to write his weekly sermon must be given some idea of how he can or cannot legitimately handle his text for the week. The method he uses must grow out of the real nature of the Scriptural material with which he is dealing. John Bright began the presentation of valid methodology in his book *The Authority of the Old Testament*.[5] Brevard Childs considerably enlarged the

20

discussion in *Biblical Theology in Crisis*. But many more models must be furnished the local preacher, and such models must be related to concrete characteristics of the Biblical text.

It is with these needed steps in recovering our Biblical heritage in the church that this volume is concerned, and the discussion follows according to the last three steps listed above. Obviously it would be reckless folly and blind arrogance to claim that this book covers the entire subject or even attempts to do so. Most of the Biblical theologians in the Western world are concentrating on the third step of formulating adequate hermeneutical principles, for example, and it will take the combined work of the leaders of the church in all its manifestations to unite congregations with the Bible again. In addition, this book deliberately concentrates upon the author's special field of competence—that of interpreting the Old Testament as the word of God in the twentieth century. Because the basic mode of interpreting the Word of God has been and remains proclamation, major attention is given in the book to preaching and its method. Nothing is said about the use of the Old Testament in a teaching context, although it is hoped that this volume will serve to make Christian educators more aware of what they are doing with the Scriptures.

If this work aids at all in the ongoing discussion of the use of the Bible in the church, or if it aids just one pastor in one lonely outpost of Christendom in preaching the word of God in Jesus Christ to his people on one Sunday of the year, then the author's labor will have been abundantly rewarded.

Chapter II

How the Old Testament
Was Lost

I F WE WANT to recover the Bible in American Protestantism, we must become aware of how we lost it in the modern era in the first place, and it is this subject with which this chapter will attempt to deal.[1]

To understand our present situation, we must begin our story three centuries back with the church's attitude toward the Bible in the century after the Reformation. In the post-Reformation world of the seventeenth century, the Bible had a well-defined place within the life of the church. It was viewed as the main support for orthodox dogmatic theology. It had become necessary in the Protestant Church to secure the results of the Reformation in the dogmatic systems of the church, and while the Reformers had used dogmatics to present the teachings of the Bible, this program was now reversed. Now the Bible was used to support dogmatic statements.

As a result, the Bible was understood as a collection of proof texts. Little or nothing was understood of its history, and thus it was viewed as a collection of isolated truths and teachings which could be made to support one or another Protestant theology of the day. Passages were torn from their contexts and given fully alien meanings. Old Testament texts were understood merely as types of the New. Inspiration was interpreted in a very rigid manner, and the Bible was understood as an absolutely infallible book, containing neither contradictions nor progress.

In short, the Bible was made completely subservient to the dogmatic systems of the day, in much the same manner as can still be seen in modern fundamentalism. It could be made to support almost any theological position, because it was in reality the dogmatic system and not the Bible that was the supreme authority.

Yet, as is also true in modern fundamentalism, there was a vital interest in the Bible in this period. With respect to the Old Testament, every detail of the cult, of Old Testament anthropology, and of archaeology was avidly received and studied, but all because it might give support to the dogmatic theology of the day.

Obviously it was necessary that the study of the Bible be freed from the confining boundaries of dogmatics, and this freedom was gained in the rationalism of the Enlightenment.

In the Enlightenment, in every discipline, man was freed from the authority of scholastic systems, to become the measure of all things, and the tool which the Enlightenment used to measure all things was man's own sovereign reason. Reason was applied to law and economics, to art and science, to history and philosophy—and to the study of the Scriptures.

This movement was prepared for as early as the time of Thomas Hobbes (1588–1679) and Baruch Spinoza (1632–1677). Both of these philosophers maintained that reason had the right to judge the Scriptures, apart from the tradition of the church. The Scriptures are not God's revealed word, maintained Hobbes, but merely the record of the men who received the revelation, and thus the Scriptures could be subject to rational interpretation.[2]

It was in the eighteenth century, however, that Rationalism reached full flower, and in the field of Biblical interpretation it was men such as A. F. Buesching and J. S. Semler and, above all, Johann Philipp Gabler who led the way in separating Biblical interpretation from the confining limits of dogmatics. In 1787, Gabler gave his inaugural address at the University of Altdorf, entitled "Academische Rede de iusto discrimine theologiae biblicae et dogmaticae," in which he advocated that Biblical theology be separated from dogmatic theology as an objective, historical discipline in itself, dedicating itself to what Biblical writers thought about divine matters. To separate the two disciplines, said Gabler, Biblical study should be pursued in three steps: first, the Biblical theologian should interpret individual passages, using purely grammatical and historical principles; second, he should compare passages, noting their points of agreement and disagreement; third, he should formulate general ideas about the passages without distorting them or obliterating their diversity. On the firm basis of this scientific study of the Bible, then, the dogmatic theologian could erect a superstructure of dogmatic theology directed to the needs of his own time.[3]

This whole program was given enormous impetus by the beginnings of textual, literary, and historical criticism of the Bible, and with the publications of Johann Gottfried Eichhorn's *Introduction to the Old Testament* in 1780–1783, sound principles of Biblical criticism, freed from dogmatics, were introduced in a decisive manner into Biblical interpretation. Indeed, using such principles, both W. A. Teller[4] and W. F. Hufnagel[5] began to use the Bible as a canonical tool to criticize dogmatic orthodoxy. Wrote Hufnagel, "The proof texts must be used to correct the theological system, not the system the proof texts."[6]

Rationalism decisively showed that the Bible could not possibly be reduced to a unified handbook of dogmatic instruction without doing violence to it, and instead, it contented itself with describing the various ideas and teachings of the different Biblical writers. In this vein, two important works were issued: C. F. Ammon's *Biblische Theologie* (1792) and G. L. Bauer's large four-volume work, *Theologie des Alten Testaments* (1796). However, the major shortcomings of rationalism were its marked tendencies not only to atomize the Bible by treating it as a collection of unrelated teachings and ideas but also to-

24

tally to rationalize it and to regard only that which seemed reasonable to eighteenth-century man as of lasting value. For example, Bauer regarded all supernatural revelation of God through theophanies, miracles, and prophecies as contrary to sound reason, and much of the Old Testament he saw as only the product of the "fantastic" Oriental mind.[7]

There were, however, other movements afoot which counteracted both of these shortcomings of rationalism. In 1753, Robert Lowth had published his famous work on Hebrew poetry,[8] followed by Johann Gottfried Herder's *Vom Geist der hebräischen Poesie* (The Spirit of Hebrew Poetry), in 1782. Both of these works had emphasized the aesthetic beauty and religious feeling to be found in Hebrew literature. At the same time, Friedrich Schleiermacher (1768–1834) was setting forth his philosophy of religion as the empirical feeling of absolute dependence on God. And in 1813, W. M. L. de Wette wrote his *Biblische Dogmatik des Alten Testaments und Neuen Testaments,* in which he tried "to rise above both orthodoxy and rationalism to a higher unity of faith and religious feeling."[9] There was at the time new emphasis on religion as an expression not only of rational thought but of feeling and aesthetics and emotion as well.

Even more important, the work of George Wilhelm Friedrich Hegel (1770–1831) was a major influence in approaching the Bible not as an atomistic collection of ideas but as an organic whole. In his posthumously published *Philosophy of Religion,* Hegel maintained that religion had passed through three stages in its evolution: that of the religion of Nature, of the religion of Spiritual Individuality (Jewish, Greek, and Roman religions), and of Absolute Religion, which Hegel identified with Christianity. In 1835, Wilhelm Vatke therefore seized upon Hegel's developmental view to write his *Die biblische Theologie: Teil* I, dealing with the Old Testament. Religion develops in a historical process, said Vatke, which is an organic whole, and each part must be understood as a member of the whole. Within the Old Testament itself then, Vatke identified three stages in its evolution, each characterized by a particular ritual law. The first stage was that of primitive worship, as in the Yahwist and Elohist documents and the books of Samuel and Kings. The second stage was that of ethical consciousness, as in the Deuteronomic History and the Prophets. The third stage was that of external, ceremonial religion, as in the Levitical law of P.[10] Unfortunately for Vatke, his theories were burdened by a heavy Hegelian framework and were spurned by other Old Testament scholars, notably Heinrich Ewald, the leading Old Testament authority at the time. Vatke's work made no impression on Biblical scholarship until it was later confirmed by the work of Karl H. Graf, Abraham Kuenen, and, above all, Julius Wellhausen.

After the middle of the nineteenth century, Graf conclusively showed, building on the critical work that had gone before him, that P was the latest document in the Pentateuch and not the product of Moses. It had previously been believed that because P was connected with the Mosaic period, it was the earliest document, and the religion of Israel had been viewed as the continual struggle to maintain an ideal system of law, developed in the beginning by Moses. With the Grafian hypothesis, the way was laid for viewing the cultic legislation of Israel as the last stage in the development of its religion from a simple to a complex system of faith.

Finally, it must be pointed out that not only in the fields of philosophy and religion but also in the field of science the concepts of evolution and development were coming to the fore. In 1859, Charles Darwin published his *On the Origin of Species by Means of Natural Selection,* in which all supernatural causes of biological evolution were dispensed with and the theory of natural evolution was posited. In the following decades, the English philosopher Herbert Spencer (1820–1903) popularized the idea that the cultural history of mankind had likewise evolved, and this had a great influence on the field of anthropology. Under the leadership of Edward B. Tylor, the anthropologists maintained that all cultures had developed from the simple to the complex. Within each culture, they theorized, the earliest and most primitive state of man's religion was animism, in which primitive man attributed living essence or soul to everything about him. Out of such primitive beginnings, then, all religions developed.[11]

In philosophy, in religion, in Biblical criticism, in biological science, in anthropology, the overwhelming emphasis during the last half of the nineteenth century was on the evolution and development of man's existence, and it remained only for the genius of Julius Wellhausen to sum up the spirit of the age in his famous philosophy of Israel's history. In 1878, Wellhausen published his *Die Geschichte Israels I*, which from the second edition of 1883 onward was known as *Prolegomena zur Geschichte Israels*. This work summed up, in great detail and with comprehensive finality, the results of the scientific criticism of the Bible for the past century, and it laid the foundation for an organic understanding of the development of Israel's religion. Subsequently, in 1894, Wellhausen put out a second volume, entitled *Israelitische und jüdische Geschichte*, in which he spelled out even more fully the consequences of criticism for the interpretation of Old Testament religious history. In these two works, Wellhausen formulated a philosophy of Israel's history which determines the approach of large segments of the church toward the Bible even still today, and it is this Wellhausian philosophy which we must understand if we want to comprehend how we lost the Bible in American Protestantism.

First of all, as a man of his time, Wellhausen claimed to be dealing with his sources from a strictly scientific, objective viewpoint. He rejected all supernatural elements and causes in Israel's history, and said that it represented simply the natural development of human institutions and ideas, proceeding by its own inner dynamic and paralleling natural development and evolution in the biological world. For this reason, Wellhausen's view has often been named the "genetic view" of the Old Testament.

All of the material in the Old Testament, maintained Wellhausen, could be fitted without distortion into a neat evolutionary scheme. The history of Israel's religion began with the

27

exodus, because the lofty monotheism ascribed to Abraham could not possibly have been present in the beginning of Israel's development. There were then three stages in the development of Israel's religion:

1. There was the early natural period of monolatry, in which Israel spontaneously expressed its religious feeling in simple rituals. This was the period of animism and polydaemonism, in tribal religion, which then developed onward toward a national cultus and henotheism.

2. The second stage was that of strict monotheism, in which the relation of man to God was no longer cultic and national, but ethical and spiritual. This stage was reached through the work of the prophets and the tragedy of the exile, and was actually considered by Wellhausen to be the highest and most influential stage in Israel's development.

3. However, there followed the third stage of the cultic and legalistic religion of postexilic Judaism, as manifested in the P document. This stage was characterized by an emphasis on conformity to cultic and moralistic regulations, by the centralization of the cult, by ritualistic development, and by the formation of an ecclesiastical state. It was, in Wellhausen's view, an exceedingly creative period, giving birth to The Psalms, the Wisdom Literature, and the collection of the Old Testament as a whole. Nevertheless, this stage represented a crystallization of Old Testament teaching in which the early natural spontaneity of Israel's first stage was lost, and in which the ethical religion of the prophets was turned into strict legalism.

It was this genetic view of the Old Testament which dominated Old Testament interpretation for almost a generation after Wellhausen, and the results of this interpretation were disastrous for the church's understanding of two thirds of its canon. In this view everything that was earliest in Israel's history was automatically labeled as primitive and put at the bottom of the scale of development as having minimal worth. The story of the Old Testament was understood as the story of Israel's development out of crude and primitive beginnings through the high ethical religion of the prophets to the legalism of postexilic Judaism.

When this view was applied to the Bible as a whole—and it soon was—it meant that the whole of Biblical religion was seen as a continuing development, with the New Testament forming the peak of the process, and one's understanding of the process could be stated in one of two ways, depending upon one's point of view. Either one could say that man's ideas about God and religion developed naturally from lower to higher forms, or the theory could be stated theistically and one could say that this development represented God's progressive revelation of himself. A third alternative was to combine the two statements and say that the Biblical history as a whole represented man's progressively deeper understanding of God's progressive revelation of himself. But however stated, "history" and "development" were the magic words, and everything was understood in terms of them.

One of the typical works produced at the time was W. Robertson Smith's *History of the Religion of the Semites* (1889), in which Smith saw Israel entering Palestine with a primitive communal nomadic religion of sacrifice. Gradually however, said Smith, Israel freed herself from such materialism and communalism, and one could then find in Israel's history a progression of her ideas toward the final stage of the pure "spiritual truths" of Christianity.

Again this understanding of Israel's religious history was supported by the anthropological studies of the time.[12] Between 1890 and 1915, Sir James G. Frazer published his three editions of his classic work, *The Golden Bough,* in which he characterized all primitive religion as a religion of "dynamism" or of impersonal power permeating all. In 1918, he applied this theory to the Old Testament in his book *The Folk-lore in the Old Testament,* purporting to find in the Old Testament many survivals of primitive dynamistic belief. Thus it was believed by many that in the Old Testament there could indeed be found evidence of man's earliest and most primitive religion.

29

Similarly, between 1910 and 1928, Lucien Lévy-Bruhl carried on his investigations of pre-logical magical thought, and in 1912, Émile Durkheim issued his studies of mana as the basis of group religion.[13] The overwhelming presupposition became that one or the other of these forms of primitive religion was characteristic of Israel's earliest religious stages, and in his *Psalmenstudien* of 1922–1924, Sigmund Mowinckel added to this conviction by pointing out evidences of magic and sorcery in the religion of the psalms.

The important point is that such developmental treatments of the Old Testament resulted in the total devaluation of its worth in the church. It was considered to be simply the history of the first stages in man's spiritual evolution, whose lower ideas of God and faith had subsequently been superseded by the higher spiritual truths of Christianity. The Old Testament had no revelatory value in itself. It was simply the historical preparation for the New Testament, and although one had to know something of the Old Testament background to understand the New Testament—for example, the development of the concept of Messiah—the examination of this background was of importance only to the scholar.

This attitude was mirrored in the Biblical commentaries of the time. For example, in the old edition of the *International Critical Commentary* or in the *Handkommentar zum Alten Testament,* edited by Wilhelm Nowack and Karl Marti, only historical problems of the Old Testament were dealt with, and once they had been clarified, the discussion ended. It was felt that the Old Testament had no spiritual or theological value, and it need be dealt with only as a historical collection.

The result was that treatments of the meaning and theology of the Old Testament were no longer issued. After the publication of the fifth edition of Hermann Schultz's Old Testament theology in 1896, there were no further systematic expositions of Old Testament belief in German for twenty-five years. And in English, the last full-length Old Testament theology before 1940 was Andrew Bruce Davidson's work in 1904.

Instead, the scholarly world and the church were flooded

with a series of histories of Israelite religion. The first important one of these was Rudolf Smend's *Alttestamentliche Religionsgeschichte* in 1893, and this was followed in quick succession by similar histories by Friedrich Giesebrecht (1904), Max Löhr (1906), Karl Marti (1907), Karl Budde (1910), Eduard König (1915), Rudolf Kittel (1921), Gustav Hölscher (1922), and William O. E. Oesterley and Theodore H. Robinson (1930). Even the works that were entitled theologies of the Old Testament were in reality nothing more than expositions of a historical process, for example, the 1911 theologies of the Old Testament by Bernhard Stade and Emil Kautzsch. Moreover, all these books had basically the same theme: through human discovery, Israel freed her religion from naturalism and collectivism and rose to a progressively more ethical and individual religion. Oesterley and Robinson's 1930 book, *Hebrew Religion: Its Origin and Development,* was typical. One fourth of the book was given over to the description of Israel's animistic and magical background, from which she finally freed herself, rising through the stages of polytheism and henotheism to pure and spiritual monotheism.

The study of the message of the Old Testament had become nothing more than the study of the history of Israel's religion, and that history was viewed almost totally in developmental, naturalistic, and positivistic terms. No attention was given to Israel's own understanding of her history or to the witness of her faith. Indeed, the fact that the Bible constantly gives a theological interpretation of its history was regarded by many as regrettable and a demerit. The Old Testament's claim to revelation and authority was ignored or forgotten. If a scholar did not accept the developmental view of Israel's history, he was accused of having an unhistorical and therefore unscientific attitude.

Interestingly enough, the New Testament was undergoing similar treatment. In the famous Tübingen School of New Testament studies, led by Ferdinand Christian Baur (1792–1860), emphasis had been laid on the development of New Testament thought, and it was Baur's theory that the original simple religion of Jesus had been overlaid and corrupted by the later theologies of the Palestinian community, of Paul, and of the Johannine writings. In his 1847 lectures on New Testament theology, Baur arranged the New Testament material into a Hegelian scheme, with the teachings of the human Jesus as the Jewish thesis, Paul's theology of a supernatural Christ as the pagan antithesis, and Old Catholic theology of the second century A.D. as the synthesis. The way for this theory had been prepared somewhat by David Friedrich Strauss in his *Das Leben Jesu* (1835), in which he maintained that Jesus was nothing more than a Jewish wise man. And it was buttressed by Ernest Renan's sentimental picture of the Man of Galilee in his popular *La Vie de Jésus* (1863), by Wilhelm Bousset's identification of the Kingdom with the fatherhood of God and the brotherhood of man, by Adolf von Harnack's *Das Wesen des Christentums* (1899–1900), in which he maintained that the religion of Jesus was equivalent to a simple harmony between God and man, and by Wilhelm Wrede's denial of Jesus' messianic consciousness.[14]

The emphasis was almost totally on the "quest for the historical Jesus," and thus it was believed that all of the supernatural elements in the New Testament—angels and demons, miracles, eschatology, messianism—were later theological corruptions of an original simple picture of Jesus. If one could but get behind the theology of Paul and the Gospel writers, it was believed, behind the unfortunate eschatological and supernatural and messianic interpretations of the New Testament, one could recover the picture of that simple Master "who by precept and example propounded eternally valid teachings concerning the fatherhood of God, the infinite value of the human soul, and the present reality of God's kingdom within the hearts of all who have accepted his command to love. This was, with variations, the real Jesus of history as he was widely presented: the great teacher, the prophet, who came to tell men of the love of God and to ask them to live in love with one another." [15]

Needless to say, such a Jesus with such teachings was largely nothing more than the embodiment of the liberal Protestant ideals and morals of the time, having very little relationship to the actual witness of the New Testament. But this fictitious Jesus and his teachings were then made the measure of the worth of the Old Testament. The teachings of the simple Jesus were seen as the highest and eternally valid climax in the development of man's religion, and anything in the Old Testament which did not accord with such teachings was considered to be primitive, outdated, superseded, unchristian. The practical result was that the church ceased to use all but a few selected portions of the Old Testament—the Decalogue, some stories used as moral lessons, a few psalms, and some of the nobler sayings of the prophets. The rest of the Old Testament portion of the canon dropped from sight, as having no connection with Christianity whatsoever. It represented simply the earlier stages in man's religious development, which had now been outgrown and which could now therefore properly be discarded. In other words, for all practical purposes, American Protestantism lost the larger part of its Scriptures and returned to the heresy of Marcionism.

To be sure, the New Testament was equally being distorted. But the church in this country did not abandon the New Testament as it did the Old. It retained the belief that the New Testament contained at least valid teachings, and subsequent New Testament scholarship was able, within this framework of acceptance, to restore a more balanced presentation of the New Testament's witness to its proper position as the center of the life of the church. The Old Testament, however, was almost totally abandoned. It was considered outdated and irrelevant and invalid. It fell into almost total disuse and obscurity within the ongoing life of the church, and it has to this day never been recovered in the mainstream of American Protestantism. In the opinion of most churchgoers, there is no reason to recover it, for it is in their view the outdated document of a legalistic religion with a wrathful God, which has no connection with Christian faith.

When the church lost the Old Testament, however, it lost all possibility of fully appropriating the New Testament and its own existence as the people of God, and it opened the way for the development of that popular religious tradition which might be called "*Reader's Digest* religion," [16] which is so characteristic of American faith and practice, and yet which has so little connection with the Biblical faith. We will attempt to show in the next chapters why and how this was so.

CHAPTER III

The Results
of the Loss
of the Old Testament:
THE LOSS OF THE NEW TESTAMENT
AND THE DEVELOPMENT
OF *"READER'S DIGEST* RELIGION"

Despite his lasting contributions to the historical criticism of the Bible, Wellhausen's developmental view of Israel's history has now been thoroughly discredited within the world of Biblical scholarship.

Since the beginning of the twentieth century, archaeological and historical studies of the ancient Near East have shown that the milieu out of which Israel emerged in the Middle and Late Bronze Ages was by no means culturally and religiously "primitive." Rather, there existed in the Mediterranean world, from the third millennium on, societies with the most complex political and religious structures, and Israel has to be understood in relation to these societies. A "primitive," "animistic," "prelogical" Israel in the midst of such a world would have been an anomaly, and in fact, never did exist.

Further, during the decades of this century, Biblical scholars have convincingly shown that it is impossible to arrange the Biblical writings in a neat chronological and evolutionary scheme. Through the work of form criticism, the basic literary "documents" of the Bible, with which developmentalism

35

worked, have now been shown to be amazing and complicated arrays of old and new traditions all mixed together, gathered into various tradition complexes often already in an oral stage, and given their present arrangement usually for theological or cultic, rather than historical, reasons. To divide these traditions into their separate units, to discover their original purposes and provenance, and then to see how their incorporation into the Biblical story has affected their form and purpose has been the intent of form criticism. But all scholars now recognize that the Wellhausian philosophy of Israel's history simply failed to recognize the complex nature of the "documents" with which it attempted to deal.

Finally, prompted by the publication of Karl Barth's stunning *Der Römerbrief* in 1919, and brilliantly shown the way by Walther Eichrodt in his *Theologie des Alten Testaments* (1933–1939), Biblical theologians have increasingly recognized that a purely historical and objective treatment of the Bible ignores its central message, drastically distorts its meaning, and indeed is impossible. The Bible deals with history, to be sure, but it is history born out of the experiences of faith, history that has as its central character not man, but God. That which the Bible intends to do above all else is to witness to the actions of God. Its purpose is to proclaim and to confess those actions. Thus, when Wellhausianism purported to deal with the Biblical history as the account of the natural evolution of man's religious ideas and institutions, it ignored the basic character of the history with which it was dealing. A developmental, genetic view of the Biblical history has now been totally discredited and rejected throughout the scholarly world.

The difficulty is that the average layman, and indeed most pastors, have never absorbed this fact, and this is one of the reasons why the Biblical Theology Movement made no lasting impression on the ongoing life of the church in this country. That Movement was built on the twentieth-century Biblical scholarship outlined above, but the findings of such scholarship—especially of form criticism and tradition criticism—were never simply and clearly communicated to the church.

Therefore the church never had the presuppositional bases necessary to appropriate the new Biblical Theology. Instead, most Protestant church members in the United States carried on their faith and practice in the context of the old developmental view, so common to those "Bible helps" used widely throughout the land. The result was, as we have said, the loss of the Old Testament in the church, with the concomitant loss of the Bible as a whole.

Now why is this so? Why is it that the loss of the Old Testament makes it impossible for our church members to understand the New Testament and themselves as the people of God, and results finally in the loss of the total canon in the church? Why is it that the loss of the Old Testament leads instead to the emergence of an alternate, popular *"Reader's Digest* religion"?

The more carefully one studies the Old Testament, the more clearly there emerges a distinctive view of God and of his relation to man and his world which is absolutely essential to the Biblical faith.

The world does not exist in and for itself, according to the Old Testament. The creation has its origin solely in God's creative will (Gen., chs. 1 and 2), it is sustained solely by his faithfulness,[1] and it has its purpose only in the goal which God has appointed for it.[2] Thus there is no absolutizing of the structures of this world, there is no possibility of viewing nature's pattern as the pattern or source of man's life, and there is no way in which this present world can be seen as the final shape of reality.[3]

More importantly, however, in the Old Testament the world is always seen in contrast to God. The entire mythopoeic view of the ancient Near East is left behind, and God is not contained in any way in his creation, he does not emanate out of it, and he is not dependent on it. Rather, he is sovereign Lord over his creation and totally other from it.[4] The result is that the Second Commandment forbids Israel to find God represented in "anything that is in heaven above, or that is in the earth beneath, or that is in the water under the earth" (Ex.

37

20:4; Deut. 5:8), and the principal struggle of both Deuteronomy and the prophets was the struggle against the Canaanite
nature religions, with their identification of God with the
forces and processes of nature.

When the church lost the Old Testament, it therefore lost
this basic Biblical teaching concerning God's relation to his
creation, and opened the door to that naturalistic understanding of God which is characteristic of so much American piety
today. It is not unusual for our lay people in the church to
seek God in the world of nature around them, supposedly to
find him revealed in the beauty of lakes and trees, to "feel
closer to God" in a rustic retreat setting, or to send their children off to church camp to find God somehow in the woods.
Indeed, even many of our clergy could share the prayer for
the day, printed sometime ago in our local newspaper:

Teach us, O infinite God, to see Thee in all creation—in the
stars as well as in the daisies.[5]

God, for many American church members, lay and clergy alike,
is to be known first of all through the medium of the natural
world around them.

But if the natural world can contain and reveal God for
popular American religion, it follows, as it followed in Canaanite nature religion, that any part of the creation can become
transparent to the divine. And in the more sophisticated forms
of this natural religion in the American church, not only the
natural world, but art forms, music, science, natural and historical processes, in fact, the "depths" of all existence have
by extension come to be considered as media of the divine
revelation.[6]

The interesting point is what such a view of God's relation
to his world has done to the average church member's understanding of the New Testament. On the one hand, it has neces-
sitated the reduction of the New Testament proclamation to
the level of an account of natural processes. For example, in
many congregations, the resurrection of Christ has come to be
automatically equated with the revival of all life in the spring-

time. Or the healings of Jesus have been compared to the modern psychiatrist's use of tranquilizers. On the other hand, the belief that God can be revealed through his created world has led finally to the rejection of the New Testament altogether. If God is accessible through the "depths" of all existence to all who become aware of such depths and truly seek his presence, then there really is no need for the work of God in Jesus Christ. There is no gulf of sin, separating man from God, that needs to be bridged by the death and resurrection of our Lord. And there is no need to insist that it is through Jesus Christ alone that God is fully and truly revealed. For the person of natural religion, all the world lies at hand to reveal God, all existence becomes transparent to his presence, and that which alone is needed is man's awareness of the immanent divine. The loss of the Old Testament, with its doctrine of creation, leads almost inevitably to the development of a nature religion and to a concomitant loss of the New Testament as well.

There is also in the Old Testament a unique understanding of man which is absolutely essential to the Biblical faith. Like the world, man too is never understood in and of himself. He is understood only in his relation to God. He is uniquely given the image of God to exercise lordship over the earth, but his authority and power and his life itself come only from his Creator, upon whom he is dependent for all his capabilities and gifts (Gen., chs. 1 and 2).[7] Thus, man's history is the story of his turning to God or away from him,[8] and it is in this turning that man decides his ultimate destiny, whether he shall live or die. In and of himself, he has no mythopoeic power to find immortality or to claim a divine legitimization in his nature for anything he does. He is fully a historical creature, dependent on his Creator for his life, his abilities, and his definition of good.

When the church lost the Old Testament, it lost this unique understanding of man and opened the way on the one hand to a purely humanistic, and on the other to a mythic, understanding of man's nature.

39

Thus, on the one hand, there is in the American church a widespread ethical humanism, which equates the good or the will of God with the fulfillment of human needs and desires and rights.[9] This manifests itself in the widespread faith in "the worth of the individual" and in the overwhelming reliance on the psychological, social, and political sciences to define what is proper for man to do and be. Ethical standards are not drawn from the commandments of God and are not intended to make man's life an imitation of God's, as it should be according to the Biblical view.[10] Rather, ethics become synonymous with that which seems to fulfill the human personality or to preserve the wholeness of the community. Or in "situation ethics," the good becomes that which seems "loving" at the time, with the definition of "loving" drawn almost always from current cultural concepts. Thus man's life loses its transcendent base in God and becomes its own enclosed measure.

When such a humanistic view is imposed on the New Testament, as it often has been, the result is once again a reductionist understanding of the person of Christ. Jesus becomes the supreme humanistic example, simply a "man for others," the religious genius who demonstrates what it means to live in loving relations with one's fellowman. And, as was true in Wellhausian developmentalism, the New Testament ethic is made synonymous with the highest moral standards of the day, as those are found in the interpreter's particular society.

The reverse side of the church's loss of the Old Testament understanding of man has even more drastic consequences, for it ultimately results in the loss of the New Testament altogether. When man's life is cut loose from its moorings in history and man is no longer understood as a creature wholly dependent on his Creator, then the inevitable temptation is to regard man from a mythopoeic point of view as a creature with divine power and legitimization in himself. He becomes one who has absolute worth in himself, one who has an immortal soul or a divine spark in his human nature, one who can claim permanence and absolute rights for his constructions and life.

Practically, this view has manifested itself most widely in

40

the common belief, held by most church people, that every person has an immortal soul and that after death, the soul lives on in communion with God. Therefore, there is really no need for the New Testament proclamation of the resurrection of Jesus Christ. With or without him, man's immortal soul lives on, and the church's faith in eternal life through Christ is understood merely as a support for man's immortality. Death, in all of its finality and futility, is not faced, and the glad news of the resurrection is reduced to an affirmation of the immortal nature of man. In short, the heart of the New Testament's proclamation is really made unnecessary.

Furthermore, the New Testament's profound understandings of man's sin and suffering, and of judgment, are no longer comprehended. Man, with immortality in his soul, has certain inalienable rights. He has the right to a full life and a good life, and can legitimately claim them, and the necessity of God's judgment or of man's suffering is totally rejected, as a denial of that abundant life to which every human being is entitled. When such views are set up against the Lord's call, "Take up your cross and follow me," needless to say, that call becomes totally incomprehensible. As our former pastor once put it, "When we hear the command, 'Take up your cross,' our usual reply is, 'Just a minute; I'll bring the station wagon around, and we can put it in the back.'"

When the church lost the Old Testament, it also lost the Bible's unique understanding of God, and this especially has resulted in the emergence of that popular American faith which we have dubbed "*Reader's Digest* religion."

American popular religion, propagated through slick-cover periodicals, devotional works, and popular religious songs, as well as through some of our churches, is characterized by a belief in a more or less vaguely defined "mystical presence." This "presence" is called God, and depending upon the disposition of the individual worshiper, the presence may be identified with Jesus, with some ideal such as "love" or "truth," or with a numinous quality permeating the world of nature. The identity and definition of the presence are largely left up to the indi-

41

vidual worshiper, and each individual's definition is considered as valid as any other's.

Further, in such popular religion, the mystical presence makes itself felt largely in the emotional response of the worshiper, and the ideal is to become so aware of the presence that one is inspired, thrilled, emotionally awed, given a "mountaintop experience." However, to undergo such an experience, the worshiper is required to seek the presence, to want to find it, to pray to it and concentrate upon it, although it is generally acknowledged that the presence may be found anywhere. Various stimuli such as music, candlelight, a beautiful indoor or outdoor setting, or even a situation of need, may aid the worshiper in finding the presence. It is generally acknowledged that, once found, the experience of the presence can strengthen and comfort as well as thrill.

This experience of the presence in popular religion is, however, largely an individualistic experience, and while it may serve to comfort or help the individual, it makes little demand on the individual's life in society, and indeed may be separated from that life altogether. The experience of the presence remains largely private, individual, undemanding, never clearly defined, and thus it may be isolated from every other realm of the worshiper's life.

The development of such a popular *"Reader's Digest* religion" might have been much less widespread in American Protestantism if the church had vigorously taught and proclaimed the nature of the Biblical God to its adherents. But when the church lost the Old Testament, it made such a task almost impossible, for it is in the Old Testament that the foundations are laid for the Bible's whole understanding of God. God there is defined for Israel not primarily through his presence with her, but through the actions of power which he takes in relation to her. That is, Israel comes to know God not as "being" but as "doing," as one who initiates, shapes, and controls the course of her life through history, as one who is manifested in acts of power that affect her entire existence.[11] In the acts which he does in relation to Israel, however, God defines himself, and the identification of who God is becomes inseparable from the story of what he has done.[12] He is the one who has delivered an oppressed people out of Egyptian slavery, who has entered into covenant with them, who has led them for forty years through the wilderness, who has given them a land to call their own, who has appointed a Davidic king to rule over them, who has raised up prophets to guide them, who has destroyed them when they turned against him, and who has promised to renew them as his people. And the only one who can lay claim to the title of God is the one who has done these things.

Further, in these events, God has made his character clear, as one who has all power and who is holy, totally other than man, and yet as one who desires to live in fellowship with men in a relationship of love and trust. God therefore makes himself known to Israel as a distinctly personal Lord, as one who calls for her total and willing personal response to his loving Person.[13] Whenever this personal relationship is dissipated in a purely cultic exercise of religion or through legalistic understandings of obedience, Israel is deemed to be unworthy of communion with her God.[14]

Israel's relation with God is never an end in itself, nor is it ever limited to purely individualistic expressions. God acts toward Israel as a people; indeed, he himself creates Israel as a people.[15] But the reason for the creation is not merely in order that Israel may enjoy her relationship with God, but in order that through Israel, God may enter into loving fellowship with all men and thus restore to them the good life he intended for them in the beginning.[16] Mankind ruined God's good creation by its rebellion against his Lordship. God therefore sets out in Abraham to create a new people,[17] which will live as a community of righteousness and obedience and trust under his Lordship, and which will then form the germ cell of that universal people in which all nations are included.[18]

In short, in contrast to American "*Reader's Digest* religion," the Old Testament understanding of God is one in which God is always personal, always known by what he does, always actively working toward the goal of his Lordship over all men, and in that activity God demands that his covenant people obey him and trust his working in all circumstances, in order that through them he may establish his kingship over all the earth. There is nothing vague about the Biblical God. His character and desire are clearly made known; he even has a name—Yahweh. There is nothing undemanding about his relationship with his people; it calls for the most strenuous efforts toward obedience and trust in him alone. And there is nothing in his working which indifferently accepts the *status quo;* he rejects all present human constructions as provisional and demands that his people journey with him toward the goal of a new and righteous community of all men on earth. That American popular religion could degenerate into the worship of some vague, inactive, undemanding, private "presence" in the face of such Biblical witness is ample measure of the extent to which the Biblical faith has been abandoned in this country.

As we have said, it is this Old Testament understanding of God and his activity which forms the basis of the New Testament's view of Jesus Christ and his church. When the church lost the Old Testament, it therefore lost the Bible—and the Christian faith—as a whole. The present dilemma of the church is not that it has merely abandoned the Old Testament and is living and acting solely on the basis of the New. The present dilemma of the church is that it is attempting to carry on its life apart from the totality of its Scripture. It is impossible to have the New Testament without the Old Testament—that is the fact which the church has not grasped, and that is the fact which must be made fully clear.

We have shown in this chapter some partial effects of the loss of the Old Testament on the understanding of the New. But we have yet to examine closely the integral relationship between the two Testaments, and it is such an examination that alone makes fully clear how necessary the Old Testament is for the Christian faith. Consequently, in Part Two we shall examine in some detail the nature of the Old Testament and its relation to the New.

Part Two

THE NECESSITY OF THE OLD TESTAMENT FOR THE CHRISTIAN FAITH

CHAPTER IV

The Nature
of the Old Testament

IF WE EXAMINE the contents of the Old Testament as a whole,[1] we find a series of Yahweh-words, each of which announces the beginning of a new activity of Yahweh toward his people, and on the basis of these words the Old Testament may be divided into three principal tradition histories, or salvation histories, or *Heilsgeschichten*.[2] These are (1) the history in the Hexateuch; (2) the history that centers itself around the promise to David in II Sam., ch. 7, and includes the material in Judges, Samuel, Kings, and Chronicles-Ezra-Nehemiah; and (3) the history that is announced in the books of the classical prophets. Within each of these conglomerates of material are decisive words of Yahweh spoken to Israel, which color the entire presentation of the material and with which the material is primarily concerned.

To be sure, such a division of the Old Testament ignores the accepted "boundaries" of particular Old Testament documents. For example, the Deuteronomic History, which includes Samuel and Kings and which we have therefore put in the second division, undoubtedly begins with the books of Deuteronomy and Joshua, which we have included in our first division. We have thus overruled the division of the Old Testament on the basis of criticism alone, and have instead divided it on the basis of theology. We are saying that the most important factor in understanding the Old Testament as it is presented to us

47

is that we be clear about which particular word or words of God dominate each of its particular sections. It is in the light of those words that the material can best be understood.[3]

Further, it is quite clear that such a division of the Old Testament leaves out a consideration of The Psalms and the Wisdom writings, a criticism that has often been leveled at von Rad's *Old Testament Theology,* from which this division is taken. The criticism is much more relevant with regard to the Wisdom writings than it is to The Psalms, since the majority of the psalms constitute Israel's response, celebration, and perpetuation in the cult of Yahweh's acts in the three principal tradition histories. The Wisdom writings, on the other hand, do constitute a separate theological position in the Old Testament[4] and as such must be treated outside our division of the material. However, the theology of the Wisdom writings is not the major theology of the Old Testament, nor does it have major importance for the relationship of the two Testaments, and thus we shall include it in our discussion only as it bears upon the subject at hand.

If we look in turn at each of the three theological divisions of the Old Testament, we can see how they are each concerned with particular words of Yahweh.

A. THE HEXATEUCH

At the beginning of Gen., ch. 12, Yahweh calls Abram out of Mesopotamia and gives him a promise. In the original tradition, which JE preserves, this promise had a twofold content—that of land and of descendants, as recorded in Gen., chs. 12 and 15. However, in Gen. 12:3, J has recorded a third element from the tradition of the divine word—that of the promise that through Israel all the families of the earth will find blessing. And in the P version of the promise in Gen. 17:1–8, there is the further guarantee that Yahweh will establish an everlasting covenant with Abraham and his descendants, in which he will be their God (Gen. 17:8) and, by implication, they will be his people.

It is significant in the Hexateuch as it now stands that these four particular gifts of Yahweh are promised, for they surely are intended to form Yahweh's answer to the history of mankind, as it is presented in the preface of Gen., chs. 1 to 11. In that preface, God's good creation is disrupted by man's rebellious attempt to be his own god and by God's ensuing judgment on such rebellion. The result is that mankind loses his paradise and its fruitfulness, all forms of human community become impossible, and the intimate communion which the creature man was to know with his Creator God is changed into a relationship in which all the earth stands under God's wrath. The promise to Abraham then forms the direct response to this. Abraham is promised a new land, which in the traditions that follow increasingly takes on the shape of a paradise (cf. Deut. 8:7–10). He is told that he will become the father of a new community, through which God's wrath on all mankind will be turned into blessing. And he is promised that God will restore his relationship with such community in an eternal covenant. Israel's particular history is thereby understood as God's response to the sinful rebellion of mankind as a whole, and Abraham and his descendants are invested with worldwide significance.

The decisive question of the Hexateuchal tradition history is therefore, Has God kept his promise? Has he kept his word which bears such importance for all mankind, and if so, how?

The answers that the Hexateuchal history supplies to these questions are woven out of the most varied types of tradition, gathered together from the most widely diverse settings—cult legends, patriarchal sagas, Wisdom Literature, prophetic songs, priestly legal writings, Canaanite legal and cultic practices, desert traditions, and so forth. But out of all the diversity of the traditions used, there emerges the one story of the faithfulness of Yahweh to his word.

First Yahweh struggles with the obstacles to his promise of

descendants—with Sarah's entrance into the Pharaoh's harem (Gen. 12:10–20; cf. chs. 20:1–18; 26:1–11), with the old age of Abraham and his wife (Gen. 18:11), with the barrenness of Rebekah (Gen. 25:21) and Rachel (Gen. 30:1 ff.), with the threat to the life of Jacob, the bearer of the promise, from both Esau and Laban, with the famine which threatens the life of his tiny people in the time of Joseph, with the slaughter of the boy babies by the Pharaoh of Egypt (Ex., ch. 1). To tell this story, a thousand human incidents of jealousy and greed and power and love are woven together. But through them all, Yahweh preserves his promise and his people, until Exodus can note, "The people multiplied and grew very strong" (Ex. 1:20).

Yahweh cannot give a people a land, however, when that people is enslaved in Egypt, and so the story of the exodus is set into the context of God's remembrance of "his covenant with Abraham, with Isaac, and with Jacob" (Ex. 2:24; cf. Deuteronomy's similar recollection in Deut. 7:8), just as is the story of the long guidance in the wilderness (cf. Deut. 8:1–10). And the story of the conquest under Joshua, then, becomes the final confirmation of the promise, so that the D editor can note near the end of Joshua:

> Thus the LORD gave to Israel all the land which he swore to give to their fathers; and having taken possession of it, they settled there. (Josh. 21:43.)

In P's version of the promise, with its guarantee of the special relationship or covenant of Israel with God (Gen. 17:1–8), P understands this part of the promise to have been fulfilled on Sinai, with the giving of the covenant commands through Moses and the descent of the glory of Yahweh to the tabernacle (Ex. 40:34 ff.). In the Sinai traditions as they now stand, this is harmonized with the JE version of the actual covenant ceremony in Ex. 24:1–11, and with the insertion of the Ritual Decalogue (Ex., ch. 34) and the Covenant Code (Ex. 20:22 to 23:33) into JE, as well as with the insertions of H (Lev., chs. 17 to 26) and much of the legislation of Leviticus and Numbers into P. But the theological result of this harmonization is the affirmation of the faithfulness of Yahweh to his promise, in the establishment of his covenant with Israel on Sinai. Yahweh becomes Israel's God and Israel becomes his people. The covenant is cut, or made, and Yahweh thereby keeps his word.

As for J's addition to the promise in Gen. 12:3, that through Israel all the families of the earth shall be blessed, this remains the one element in the promise given to the patriarchs which finds no fulfillment in the Hexateuchal tradition history itself. It is certainly a prominent element in the patriarchal tradition, being reiterated for Abraham in Gen. 18:18 and 22:18, and then passed on to Isaac (Gen. 26:4) and Jacob (Gen. 28:14; cf. ch. 27:29), as the heirs of the promise. Further, there are echoes of the tradition in the story of Joseph, whose presence in Potiphar's house brings blessing upon that Egyptian (Gen. 39:5), and the ancient oracle of Balaam in Num. 24:3–9 gives voice to the same tradition as that contained in Gen. 12:3a. But any real fulfillment of this part of the word of Yahweh is left open in the Hexateuch, a development that seems strange in the light of the fact that this promise of blessing is so necessary after the history of Yahweh's cursing in Gen., chs. 2 to 11. We do not hear again of Gen. 12:3 until we come to the prophetic eschatology,[5] and then the prophets recall this ancient word (Isa. 19:24–25; 44:3; Jer. 4:2; Zech. 8:13; Mal. 3:12), as they recall so much of the Hexateuchal tradition.

Further, the nonfulfillment of this part of the promise to the patriarchs seems of little interest to the Hexateuchal theologians. The D Historian, in Joshua, can survey the past of Israel from the time of the call of Abraham until the settlement in the Promised Land, and declare that Yahweh has kept all his words and brought his salvation history to an end:

Not one of all the good promises which the LORD had made to the house of Israel had failed; all came to pass. (Josh. 21:45; cf. ch. 23:14.)

This is the theological witness which dominates the variety of the Hexateuch—the confession that Yahweh has acted through

51

all the vicissitudes of Israel's history, to keep his word to the Fathers. And it is that word, then, that promise first spoken to Abraham, which colors and shapes the content and arrangement of the first six books of the Old Testament.

B. THE MONARCHICAL TRADITIONS

When we come to the second major theological complex of the Old Testament, the material of Judges-Nehemiah, we find equal concern with a central, determinative word of Yahweh and its working. The conception is that the salvation history of the Hexateuch has come to an end. In other words, that word has been fulfilled. A new era is now entered, that of the time in the land, and appropriate to the new era is a new action of Yahweh, begun by his word spoken into Israel's history and then carried forward by that word.

Unlike the word in the Hexateuchal history, the new word of Yahweh is not spoken immediately at the beginning of the new era. There is the preparatory time of the Judges and of Saul, when Israel's inability either to remain faithful to Yahweh or to protect herself, especially against the Philistine threat, becomes apparent, and the miscarriage of Saul's reign makes it very clear that a king will rule in Israel only by Yahweh's word.[6] The one who is chosen through the word of Yahweh given to the prophet Samuel is David (I Sam. 16:1–13), and David's rise to power is seen as the result of the success Yahweh bestows upon him (I Sam. 18:14; II Sam. 5:10; *et al.*). But then, when David has risen to the height of his power and is installed in Jerusalem as king over all Israel, the decisive word is spoken (II Sam., ch. 7). David is promised, through the prophet Nathan, that his throne "shall be established for ever" (II Sam. 7:16), that Yahweh will raise up for David after him offspring, who will succeed to his throne (II Sam. 7:12) and from whom Yahweh will never withdraw his covenant love (II Sam. 7:15),[7] that Yahweh will adopt the Davidic king as his son (II Sam. 7:14), and that because of Yahweh's covenant with the Davidic king, Israel will dwell secure (II Sam. 7:10–11) as the people of God (II Sam. 7:24). In short, it is affirmed that the faithless people of the time of the Judges are nevertheless related now to Yahweh in a new way, through his eternal covenant and love toward the house of David. The divine rejection of the monarchy, which haunted the reign of Saul, is gone, and Yahweh now sets out on a new course in a new relationship with his people.

1. *The Succession Narrative*

In the material that follows this climactic announcement, all attention is focused on the promise of a Davidic heir, and the so-called Succession Narrative of II Sam., ch. 6, to I Kings, ch. 2, takes as its principal theme the question, Who will sit on David's throne after him? The theological structure of the story is remarkably similar to that of the story of Abraham. Both accounts begin with the notice of the childlessness of the bearer of the promise (II Sam. 6:23; Gen. 15:2), and both concern themselves first of all with the way in which Yahweh keeps this part of his promise. But the stories give totally different pictures of the manner of Yahweh's working. In the Genesis sagas, Yahweh intervenes through miraculous actions and revelations and cultic mediations to keep his word. In the Succession Narrative, his action is so hidden as to be almost imperceptible. The remarkable eyewitness accounts of the Succession Narrative deal with David's lust for Bathsheba and his murder of Uriah, with Amnon's rape of Tamar and Absalom's murder of Amnon, with Absalom's revolt against his father, and the tragic events of Absalom's death, with the intrigues of Adonijah and his cohorts Abiathar and Joab. There is nothing miraculous in the stories and they certainly are not religious or sacral. But it is precisely in the midst of this profane and troubled history that the author sees Yahweh working, through the lusts and greeds and ambitions and fears of the human heart. After the birth of Solomon to the adulterous David and Bathsheba, the author gives us the half-sentence that the Lord loved Solomon

(II Sam. 12:24). All that follows therefore works out to confirm this divine love, so that one by one the other aspirants to the throne of David are eliminated by their own murky dealings, and at the end of the story, Solomon, the beloved of God, succeeds to his father's throne (I Kings 2:46). The implications are that Yahweh has used the evil of man to work out his will, and that Solomon is placed on the throne of David in fulfillment of the promise.

2. The Deuteronomic History

The Succession Narrative, with its remarkable understanding of the working of God, now stands in the Old Testament, however, as an integral part of the Deuteronomic History (Deuteronomy to II Kings), and if we are to maintain our thesis that the promise to David forms the focal point around which the material in Judges-Nehemiah is centered, then we also have to show how and why II Sam., ch. 7, is central for the D Historian. (We shall come to the Chronicler a little later.)

The Deuteronomic History is written in the light of the exile, probably about 550 B.C. and probably in Palestine. It concerns itself primarily with the quandary of why the tragedies of 722 and 586 B.C. have taken place, and the answer given to this question focuses sharply on Israel's attitude over against the word of God.

As we saw in dealing with the Hexateuch, the presupposition of the D Historian is that, with the settlement into the land, the salvation history initiated with the fathers had come to an end. The end of that era is summed up by the D Historian in the speech of Joshua in Josh., ch. 23. However, as is also evident in that speech, the D Historian saw the time following the settlement in the land in a specific light. It was Israel's time of testing (cf. Judg. 3:4), the time when it would be made clear whether Israel would love the Lord with a whole heart by walking in his commandments or whether she would turn aside to other gods and become like the people who remained around her in the land. In short, for the D Historian, Israel's entrance

54

into the land set her before a decision between life and death, blessing and curse (cf. the summarizing D statement in Deut., ch. 30). If she loved the Lord with all her heart, "by walking in his ways, and by keeping his commandments and his statutes and his ordinances," then she would live and multiply, and the Lord would bless her in the land. But if her heart turned away,[8] so that she went after other gods, then she would be cursed by Yahweh and perish from the land.

This promise of blessing or curse, of life or death, stood for the D Historian, in the ancient preaching of Deuteronomy (cf. Deut., chs. 27 and 28). It was the word of God which Moses had delivered to Israel before the entrance into the Promised Land, and like every other word of God, it had to be fulfilled. The D Historian therefore set himself the task of showing how this word had been fulfilled.

His initial conclusion was that in the time of the Judges, which the D Historian considered to extend through the time of Samuel (I Sam., ch. 12), Israel repeatedly failed her test and thus fell victim to the judgment of God, inflicted on her through the instrument of warfare with her neighbors (cf. the D summary of the period of the Judges in Judg. 2:11–23). During this period, Yahweh continually showed his patience with his apostate people by heeding their cries of repentance and raising up for them deliverers. But their faithlessness rose to its final heights in their demand for a king (I Sam. 12:12), in order that he might lead them in warfare and they might be "like all the nations" (I Sam. 8:5). Nevertheless, Yahweh once again dealt patiently and mercifully with his people and gave them a king. But his word through Samuel at the close of the era of the Judges was that his patience was not inexhaustible. Israel was still being tested as the monarchy began:

If you still do wickedly, you shall be swept away, both you and your king.

This view is set forth in I Sam., ch. 12 (v. 25), in one of those summarizing speeches which are so characteristic of D and which mark D's reflections on the course of Israel's history.[9]

Israel still faces, as she begins the monarchy, the choice between life and death, and it is Yahweh's mercy alone that has kept her alive to make this choice once again.

Saul utterly fails the test. In both accounts of his rejection (I Sam., chs. 13 and 15), his failure is that of disobedience to the word of God,[10] which word the D Historian sees as decisive for the course of Israel's history. Moreover, in I Sam. 15:29, an ominous note is sounded: God will no longer show patience in fulfilling his word of judgment, and the result of this is the downfall and death of Saul. Israel's king is swept away, as Samuel had said he would be.

Meanwhile David has risen to power, and there follows then his enthronement as king over all Israel and the divine promise given through Nathan (II Sam., ch. 7). With this promise, the D Historian considers his history to have reached its watershed. On the one hand, Israel's entire previous time in the land has been marked by failure. On the other, there now emerges at this climactic moment the one who does not fail. David is, in the D Historian's view, the one whose heart is wholly true, the one who keeps the law of Deuteronomy by loving the Lord and walking in his statutes and commandments (I Kings 11:38), the one who follows Yahweh with all his heart and does only that which is right in Yahweh's eyes (I Kings 14:8).[11]

In view of the revealing history in the Succession Narrative, this is a surprising estimate of David,[12] but it is based upon one principal factor: David's determination in his heart to build a house for Yahweh (II Sam. 7:3) to house the Ark, which he has brought up to Jerusalem (II Sam., ch. 6), and thus to provide the permanent place where Yahweh can "put his name" and so be worshiped as present in Israel. Yahweh had promised in Deuteronomy that he would choose one place, "to make his name dwell there" (Deut. 12:5, 11), and he had commanded that henceforth all worship be centralized at that one place (Deut., chs. 12; 14:23 ff.; 16:2, 6, 11; 26:2). It is now David who desires in his heart to implement this promise, and who thus reveals that his heart is wholly true to Yahweh's word.

The response of Yahweh to this desire of his "servant David" is the promise given through Nathan (II Sam., ch. 7), in which Yahweh promises instead to make David a house (II Sam. 7:11) and thus reserves the fulfillment of his word to himself (I Kings 8:24). Not until the reign of Solomon will Yahweh put his name in Jerusalem and thus be present in the midst of his people in the Temple (I Kings 8:13). Nevertheless, because of David's faithfulness to the word of Deuteronomy, Yahweh enters into an eternal covenant with the house of David and guarantees Israel's existence under her Davidic king.[13] With Solomon's dedication of the Temple, the D Historian therefore considers that a twofold promise has come to pass: Yahweh has raised up an heir after David to sit upon his throne, as he promised in II Sam., ch. 7, and he has put his name in Jerusalem, as he promised in Deuteronomy. These fulfillments therefore guarantee Israel's existence in the land,[14] and Solomon sums up this fulfillment in his final speech at the dedication of the Temple, just as Joshua had summed up the fulfillment of the earlier patriarchal era in his final words (Josh. 23:14):

> Blessed be the LORD who has given rest to his people Israel, according to all that he promised; not one word has failed of all his good promise, which he uttered by Moses his servant. (I Kings 8:56.)

But Israel does not remain in the land. As the D Historian writes in the time of the exile, the Northern Kingdom has disappeared from history, and Judah is in ruins, her leading citizens in captivity. The D Historian's purpose remains to show why this has come about.

The answer which follows in the books of Kings is that the heirs to the throne of David have not walked in the example of that monarch, they have not obeyed the word of Deuteronomy and worshiped Yahweh only in the Temple in Jerusalem, where he has caused his name to dwell.[15] Instead, they have fostered idolatrous worship at the high places throughout the land, and thus have turned Israel and Judah aside to the worship of Canaanite and other pagan gods.[16] It is for this reason, says the D Historian, that destruction and exile have come upon Israel and Judah—their kings have made them sin: their kings, who were to be the guarantee of their existence in the land because of the promise to David, have not followed the word of God. Thus Yahweh's judgment has come upon his chosen people, as Deuteronomy had said it would. The people have perished from off the land, and Yahweh's judgment has been entirely just.

But in the D Historian's view, that is not the whole story. There yet remains Yahweh's promise to David, through Nathan, that there would never fail an heir to sit on David's throne, the promise that Yahweh would keep an everlasting covenant with David, and, through David, with his people. Yahweh had added something to his word beyond Deuteronomy. He had added the word to David in II Sam., ch. 7, and that word too must be fulfilled.[17] It is thus the word to David which becomes the basis of the D Historian's hope in the time of the exile, and it is finally that word which he holds up before his captive people. At the close of his history, in 561 B.C., he reports the news that the Davidic heir, Jehoiachin, has been released from prison in Babylon (II Kings 25:27–30). The import is that the Davidic heir, who can guarantee the existence of Israel, yet lives and dines at the Babylonian king's table. Through him, God can still keep his promise to David. Through him, the eternal covenant with David still stands. The D Historian does not know what the future holds or how God will keep his word. He believes only that the word of God to David must be fulfilled.

The D Historian buttresses this hope, moreover, by incorporating the Succession Narrative almost unchanged into his history. Despite the testing of Israel in the time of the monarchy and the fulfillment of the word of judgment upon Saul, D sees that a new element has entered history with the promise to David. And the grace shown to David in the gift of an heir, despite David's sin, as reported in the Succession Narrative, serves a parabolic function for the D Historian. In that document Yahweh has kept his word to David, despite David's failure. The D Historian therefore uses the story to buttress his faith that Yahweh will keep his word to David in the time of the exile, despite the failure of most of Israel's kings. The D Historian is not concerned with the fact that the Succession Narrative's picture of David directly contradicts his own. The important point for him is that there is now a new element of promise at work in history, beyond the word of Deuteronomy—the promise to David. And that promise becomes finally for the D Historian decisive for Israel's hope.

Theologically, the Deuteronomic History embodies some of the most complex views in the Old Testament. Yet the whole history centers around that which the D Historian considers to be the motive power behind the movement of history—around the working of the word of God as that word is recorded first in Deuteronomy and then most decisively in II Sam., ch. 7.

The D Historian is not alone in considering the working of the word of God to be the decisive factor in history. It was in the working of that word that Israel as a whole found her understanding of history. History consisted, for Israel, in the time between the announcement of Yahweh's promise and the fulfillment of it. It was the movement forward of Yahweh's effective word toward its goal that gave Israel her unique sense of the unity and linear nature of time. And in the second great division of the Old Testament, which we have been examining, it is the word to David that holds the center of attention.

3. *The Chronicler*

Yahweh's promise to David also holds the center of attention in the Chronicler's work, which encompasses I and II Chronicles, Ezra, and Nehemiah. In fact, the interpreter is almost led to ask what else there is central to Chronicles besides the promise to David. The Chronicler is compiling the first apology for Judaism, and his purpose is to show that in the time in which he writes (ca. 400 B.C.), true religion and indeed the center of the Kingdom of God are to be found in the tiny subprovince of Judah and not in the north among the Samaritans. Moreover, as a member of the Levitical temple guild of singers, he is at pains to elevate the role of the Levites in the cultic life of Judah.[18] But the means by which he chooses to set forth this apologetic all center around David. True religion centers in Judah and her cult because they have been founded by David, the spotless, holy king who was the chosen of Yahweh (I Chron., ch. 17).[19] It is David, in the role of a second Moses, who is the instigator of the building of the Temple (I Chron., chs. 22 ff.), who collects all the materials and holds a freewill offering for its building, and who has the plans which he hands over to Solomon (I Chron. 28:11 ff.). It is David who is the founder of the cult (cf. II Chron. 8:14 f.), who organizes the priesthood and Levites and assigns them their separate duties (I Chron., chs. 23 ff.), who sets up the singers' and musicians' guilds for the service of the Temple (I Chron., chs. 25; 15:16), and composes the hymns for the service (II Chron. 7:6). And it is the fact that David has done all these things which gives the religion of Judah its legitimacy. In fact, the Chronicler knows no other election of Israel than that guaranteed by the promise to David.[20] Yahweh's relation with Israel begins only with David, and it is through the eternal covenant with David that Israel is upheld.

Israel's responsibility, according to the Chronicler, is basically to trust Yahweh (cf. II Chron. 20:14–17, 20; 32:7–8) and to "seek him" (II Chron. 15:1–7), but this trust and seeking are understood by the compiler finally to consist in the proper exercise of the cultic duties established by David for the Temple in Jerusalem (II Chron. 13:4–12). It is there that the Kingdom of God is centered, in a kind of "realized eschatology" (II Chron. 13:8), and it is through David's heirs and the cult he has established that Israel is maintained.

The fact that the Chronicler compiles such a message in the Persian age, when Judah has no king and is nothing more than a tiny subprovince of the Persian empire, gives his work, despite its inner "realized eschatology," a distinct thrust toward the future. For he looks forward to the time when the promise to David, with its cultic presuppositions, will once again become reality. Obviously his message to his contemporaries is that salvation lies through the proper practice of the cult, but he looks for the time when the throne of David "shall be established for ever" (I Chron. 17:14).

4. *The Royal Psalms*

Before leaving this second great theological division of the Old Testament, we must say a few more words about the picture of David which the Deuteronomist and the Chronicler present in their histories. As we have noted, each of these compilers pictures David as the ideal perfect king, and each has his own particular reason for doing so—the Deuteronomist because of David's desire to centralize Yahweh's worship in the Temple, the Chronicler in order to support the claims of Judah to be the center of true religion. But another factor is at work here in the ideal picture of David which we have not noted, and this is the idealization of the Davidic office in Judah, mirrored most clearly for us in the royal psalms.[21]

As these psalms evidence, there grew up in Judah, following the time of the promise to David, a kind of "exegesis" of that promise, which drew out a picture of the ideal Davidic monarch and which was then applied, not so much to each particular incumbent of the Davidic throne, but to the office of kingship itself. Apparently the principal source of this exegesis was the court prophets, whose oracles are scattered throughout the royal psalms.[22]

In the ideal picture of the kingship which these royal prophets drew, the Davidic heir was the adopted son of Yahweh (Ps. 2:7), a man "raised on high" (II Sam. 23:1), who then enjoyed a unique relationship with Yahweh. He had the privilege of free petition to the Lord (Ps. 2:8; 21:2, 4), sitting at his right hand (Ps. 110:1) and sharing in his universal rule (Ps. 2:8-11; 110:2, 5-6; 72:8-11; 18:43-45, 47; 89:25, 27). Girded and strengthened for war by Yahweh himself (Ps. 18:32-34), the monarch was enabled to conquer all his enemies (Ps. 18:1-19, 35-42, 48; 20; 21; 45:4-5; etc.).

Within Judah herself the king was the guarantor of the righteousness, the peace, the prosperity of the nation. In his life was bound up all the life of his people, so that if the king was righteous, the people were righteous, and if the king sinned, the people sinned (cf. Ps. 18:20–27). And it was the righteous king, then, who brought the full blessing of God's *shalom* upon his people (Ps. 72; cf. Isa. 32:1–2; Jer. 23:5–6).

Not surprisingly, Judah's longing for a truly righteous Davidic heir upon the throne increasingly formed a part of her expectations concerning the future, since the coming of such a Davidic ruler would restore peace and prosperity to the nation. And certainly this traditional picture of the Davidic office which grew up in Judah shapes to a large extent the picture of the original David in both the Deuteronomist's and the Chronicler's histories. David is presented there not as he actually was, as we know so well from the Samuel stories, but as he should be, as he would be, in the new David who was to come. Both D and the Chronicler strain forward toward the future, on the basis of the promise to David, as we have seen, and the glory which they expect in the future has shaped the figure of David which they see in the past. As we shall see, such future expectation becomes of greatest importance for the New Testament.

C. THE CLASSICAL PROPHETS

We must finally turn to the third great theological division of the Old Testament, that of the classical prophets. In this division we see once again new words of God, announcing new actions on Yahweh's part, as absolutely central to an understanding of the material. The prophets of Israel cannot be understood merely as champions of social justice or as mediators of a new ethical and spiritual religion. They can only fully be understood as the heralds of a new and radical inbreaking of Yahweh into Israel's life.

Each of the prophets is different, with very specific messages directed to specific situations in the Northern and Southern Kingdoms, and in a summary of the prophets' messages we would not wish the reader to forget either this variety or the concrete nature of the divine word, which is always directed to a concrete historical situation. The prophets are not preaching "eternal truths." They are announcing the specific reactions of Yahweh to specific situations in Israel. Nevertheless, the main thrusts of the prophets' preaching can be presented in summary.

1. *The Judgment*

The astounding word of God which the eighth- and seventh-century prophets announce is that Yahweh is coming in judgment to destroy his sinful people. But this judgment is not to be like Yahweh's judgments in the past. This is not to be a judgment on particular individuals, nor is it intended merely to correct Israel and to bring her back to Yahweh. Now this judgment is to be total and absolute. This judgment is intended to bring about the death of Israel as a people.

Whether one looks at the beginning of the prexilic prophetic period in Amos or at the end of it in Ezekiel, everywhere the ominous message comes through:

> The end has come upon my people Israel;
> I will never again pass by them.
> (Amos 8:2.)

An end! The end has come upon the four corners of the land. Now the end is upon you, and I will let loose my anger upon you, and will judge you according to your ways; and I will punish you for all your abominations. (Ezek. 7:2–3.)

Thus Hosea can announce that Israel is no longer Yahweh's people (Hos. 1:9). Isaiah can proclaim that Yahweh himself has hardened Judah's heart (Isa. 6:10; 29:9–10), in order that her sin may become all the more evident as her land is made "utterly desolate" (Isa. 6:11) by that divine anger which is "not turned away" and that hand which is "stretched out still" (Isa. 9:8 to 10:4). Jeremiah, resisting the verdict at every turn, must yet acknowledge that Judah can never do right (Jer. 13:23) and that therefore the divine covenant love (*chesed*) and mer-

63

cies (*rachamim*) toward Judah have been withdrawn (Jer. 16:5) and replaced by hatred (Jer. 12:7–8).

Yahweh himself comes, according to the eighth- and seventh-century prophets, to destroy his covenant people. He whistles for the fly of Egypt and "the bee which is in the land of Assyria" (Isa. 7:18), to be sure, or he calls forth as the instrument of his destruction the mysterious foe from the north (Jer. 1:13–15; 4:5 to 6:6 *passim*). But the prophets make it very clear that it is principally Yahweh himself who comes against his people, rending them like a lion and carrying them off with none to rescue (Hos. 5:14; cf. ch. 13:9), eating away at their internal structure like a moth or dry rot (Hos. 5:12; cf. Isa. 3:1–5), passing through (Amos 5:17) or standing in their midst (Amos 7:7–9; 9:1–4) "for evil and not for good" (Amos 9:4). As the one who personally destroys, he uses all his sovereign powers to summon the scourge (Isa. 28:18) and disease (Jer. 16:4) and death to crawl into the windows (Jer. 9:21), to heave up the land (Amos 8:8), to darken the sun (Amos 8:9), to send the hail and the flood (Isa. 28:17), and to call for the chaos to come against his people (Amos 9:3; Jer. 4:23–26).

> Shall I ransom them from the power of Sheol?
> Shall I redeem them from Death?
> O Death, where are[23] your plagues?
> O Sheol, where is[23] your destruction?
> Compassion is hid from my eyes.
>
> (Hos. 13:14.)

The primary message of the preexilic prophets is therefore summarized in Amos' warning, "Prepare to meet your God, O Israel!" (Amos 4:12). God comes to do away with his people, in his day of darkness and not light (Amos 5:18). Or in Ezekiel's priestly tradition, Yahweh abandons his people and leaves them to destruction and death (Ezek. 11:22–25).

The reasons for this awful and total judgment are quite clear in the prophetic works. In her social and economic attitudes (Amos 2:6–7; Isa. 1:21–23; 5:8–22; etc.), in her political behavior (Hos. 7:3–7, 8–12; Isa. 7:1–17; 30:1–5, 15; Jer. 2:14–19; ch. 22; etc.), and especially in her cultic life (Amos 5:21–24; Hos.

2:2–13; 4:4–10, 11–14; Isa. 1:10–17; 29:13–14; Jer. 2:23–28; ch. 7; Ezek., ch. 8; etc.), Israel has totally abandoned her covenant relationship with Yahweh. She has broken Yahweh's commandment for life in his covenant community, she has relied on alliances and weapons for protection rather than on the Lord, she has persistently turned to other gods or has turned the worship of Yahweh into an automatic magical act. Gone from her are all faithfulness, thankfulness, trust, love, knowledge of her God (cf. Hos. 4:1)—all those basic requirements laid upon her by the Lord of her life. The nation of Israel, as the bride of Yahweh, has become a whore (Hosea, Jeremiah, Ezekiel). Israel, as the son of Yahweh, has rebelled against his Father (Hos. 11:1–2; Isa. 1:2–3; 30:9; Jer. 3:19–20). Whores and incorrigible sons were put to death in Israel (cf. Deut. 21:18–21; 22:13–23). Israel's behavior as a people will bring on the nation that deserved end.

The confounding element in this prophetic announcement is that it entirely cuts off the saving benefits of Israel's previous history with Yahweh. The prophets are proclaiming that neither the promise to the patriarchs nor the promise to David, neither the Hexateuchal traditions nor those of the Davidic monarchy and Zion, have any saving validity any longer in God's way with his people. The land and nationhood promised to Abraham's descendants will now be taken away. The covenant of Sinai now is abrogated and Israel is no longer God's people. The role of Israel in the midst of the earth, far from being a source of blessing, will be to become "a reproach and a taunt, a warning and a horror, to the nations round about" her (Ezek. 5:15). As for the Davidic king, he too will be judged and taken away (cf. Hos. 13:9–11; Isa. 22:25; Jer. 22:28–30; Ezek. 21:24–27). Jerusalem will be leveled into a heap of ruins (cf. Micah 3:12; Jer. 7:14), and the Temple will be destroyed (Ezek. 24:15–24).

In short, Israel can no longer look to her past with Yahweh for her confidence in the future, an exercise in which she had undoubtedly indulged in the time of the monarchy,[24] and indeed an exercise that previously had always formed the basis of Israel's hope.[25] The prophets too look to the past, recounting the tradition histories and fully acknowledging the covenantal and monarchical traditions. The difference between the prophets and the people, however, is that the people see their past with Yahweh as the basis of their future hope and life; the prophets see the past only as further proof of Israel's sin and deserved judgment. Against the background of the story of Yahweh's love and care and discipline, they set the people's persistent rebellion (Amos 2:9–11; 4:6–11; Hos. 11:1–3; Isa. 5:1–7; 1:2), and the very fact of the election increases the necessity for the judgment (Amos 3:2). Israel's past, in the recounting of the prophets, becomes part of the evidence against her in Yahweh's indictment, with even the patriarchs judged to have been guilty of rebellion (cf. Hos. 12:2–4). Ezekiel carries this radical reassessment of Israel's past with Yahweh to its final extreme, until even Israel's time in Egypt becomes a time of rebellion and idolatry, and Israel's entire history is understood as ruined with sin (Ezek., chs. 20; 16; 23).

Consequently, the sin which the prophets see present in Israel in their time is but the final manifestation of that sin which has been present in Israel from the beginning, and all of Israel, past, present, and future, is related by her common rebellion against God. It is this thoroughgoing rebellion which Yahweh meets, according to the prophetic writings, with his thoroughgoing judgment, and the prophets understand that no promise of Yahweh's in the past can avert the destruction of Israel, which is now seen as absolutely necessary (cf. Jer. 7:16–19, 20, 21–26). The previous tradition histories are of no use now in saving Israel. That is the unique and terrifying announcement of the eighth- and seventh-century prophets.[26]

2. The Hope

The hope which the prophets hold out to Israel is therefore a hope that is built, not on Yahweh's past promises to Israel, but on a totally new act of Yahweh in the future. This newness is emphasized most strongly by Second Isaiah (Isa. 43:18 f.;

cf. chs. 48:6; 54:4; 65:17), who admonishes his people to "remember not" the past saving acts of Yahweh and to look instead to Yahweh's "new thing" in the future. But all the prophets announce the totally new and future act of Yahweh which is to come, on the other side of the judgment of his people.[27]

The prophets really do not envision Israel's ability to recover from the judgment of Yahweh without this new act. For this reason, the concept of a remnant in the prophetic preaching is rather fragmentary and uncertain. Amos preaches that the Lord may be gracious to a few in the north if they will amend their ways (Amos 5:14-15, 6; cf. Zeph. 2:3), but he is equally convinced that actually nothing of the people will be left (Amos 3:12; cf. Isa. 30:13-14; 17:4-6). Isaiah names his child "A remnant shall return" (Isa. 7:3), but the promise of a remnant is really more threat than comfort (Isa. 10:20-23; 30:17; 1:9), a warning that Yahweh will indeed "make a full end, as decreed, in the midst of all the earth" (Isa. 10:23). Jeremiah attaches his hopes to the exiles of the 597 B.C. captivity (Jer. 24:4-6), but they will have to undergo a new creation (Jer. 24:7), as we shall see (cf. Jer. 29:12-14). Ezekiel sets aside those "who sigh and groan over all the abominations that are committed" in Jersualem (Ezek. 9:4), but there is no other mention of them in the judgment that engulfs Jerusalem (cf. Ezek., chs. 5; 21:3-5). By the time we reach the period of Trito-Isaiah, it is expected that there will be a chosen few within Israel who will be saved because of their righteousness (Isa. 65:8-10, 13-15), but their salvation is set within the context of a radical new creation (cf. Isa. 65:17 ff.), as is true of the remnant also in Haggai (cf. Hag., ch. 2) and Zechariah (cf. Zech., ch. 8).[28]

Everywhere the prophets announce that Yahweh's salvation of his people depends on a divine action which is yet to come, and this announcement of a "new thing" is also part of the uniqueness of the prophets' message.

If we ask about the nature of the new action of Yahweh in the future, we must say that it concerns primarily the re-creation of Israel. For at least two of the prophets, both of the exile, Israel has died before the destroying wrath of her Lord (Ezek. 37:1–4; Isa. 53:7–9), and the only way she can be restored to life is by the action of the Word and the Spirit (Ezek. 37:7–14; Isa. 52:12; 53:10–12; cf. chs. 42:1; 40:8; 55:11). Unless Yahweh raises up Israel to new life, she has no hope or future.

The other prophets do not put it in such radical terms, but they proclaim nevertheless that Yahweh must drastically transform his sinful people, if Israel is to be enabled to live before her righteous God. This transformation is pictured in several different ways.

In some of the prophetic preaching, there is the thought that the burning judgment of Yahweh will serve a purging and purifying function, smelting away all Zion's "dross" and removing her "alloy" (Isa. 1:25; cf. Ezek. 22:18–22; Isa. 48:10), melting away her "filthiness" and consuming her "rust" (Ezek. 24:9–11), washing away her "filth" and cleansing the "bloodstains" from her (Isa. 4:4), until those who are left in Jerusalem can be called holy to the Lord (Isa. 4:3). This purging and purification will get rid of Israel's idolatry (Hos. 2:17; Micah 5:12–14; cf. Isa. 27:9) and purge her proud (Zeph. 3:11; Isa. 2:6–21) and fools (Isa. 35:8) and rebels (Ezek. 20:37–38) from her midst, so that those who are left are "a people humble and lowly," who "seek refuge in the name of the Lord" and "do no wrong" (Zeph. 3:12–13). In other words, to some extent the judgment itself serves as a means to salvation. It purges and cleanses Israel until she is free of her evil (cf. Zech., ch. 5) and fit to live before Yahweh. All the prophets make it clear that Israel's first task is to accept this destruction of her evil as absolutely just and necessary.[29]

Similar to this purifying function of the judgment is the thought that it will serve Israel as a discipline and training (cf. Isa. 28:9–13). For "many days," Israel will undergo the privation of the judgment and exile, living without leaders or cult, until she learns to return and seek Yahweh and come in obedience to him (Hos. 3:4–5).

But the purification and discipline wrought by the judgment are not sufficient in themselves, in the prophets' thought, to work a thoroughgoing transformation in Israel.[30] Israel's hope, in the Old Testament, rests not on the wrath of God but on his love, and Israel has a future, according to the prophets, not because of what she may become but because of what Yahweh will do.[31] Therefore, beyond the purifying effect of the judgment, beyond the repentance of Israel, in the midst of Yahweh's wrath and indeed despite it, the prophets announce that Yahweh cannot give up his people (Hos. 11:8–9; Jer. 31:20) and will come to transform them totally. In Hosea, Yahweh will woo Israel once again (Hos. 2:14), like a young man courting his lover, and bestow a betrothal upon her in which Israel is made righteous and just, faithful to the covenant and merciful, full of the knowledge of her divine husband (Hos. 2:19–20; cf. ch. 14:4–8). In Jeremiah, Yahweh will give Israel a new heart to know and obey him (Jer. 24:7; 32:39; cf. Deut. 30:6), writing his law within the hearts of his transformed people (Jer. 31:33–34). In Ezekiel, he will thoroughly cleanse them from all their idolatry (Ezek. 36:25; 37:23) and put within them a new heart and spirit (Ezek. 36:36; 37:14; 39:29), so that Israel can walk in his covenant commandments as his re-created people.

The Isaiah traditions also understand Yahweh's transforming work in terms of the gift of the Spirit, but the recipient of the re-creating Spirit varies from tradition to tradition. Sometimes the remnant of the people receive the gift (Isa. 32:15; cf. ch. 59:21; Hag. 2:5; Joel 2:28–32), sometimes it is given to the Davidic ruler who is to come (Isa. 11:2; cf. Zech. 4:6), sometimes it is the characteristic mark of Israel personified in the figure of the Servant (Isa. 42:1).[32] Indeed, in one passage (Isa. 44:3–5), the Spirit is poured out not only on Israel but also on those of other nations, so that they too number themselves among Yahweh's covenant people.

The point is that the new Israel can come into being only by a transforming work of Yahweh, and it is upon that transforming act to come that the prophets rest Israel's hope and future. This will be the manifestation of Yahweh's forgiveness[33] and redemption[34] and salvation,[35] according to the prophets—that he will come, in a new action in Israel's history to create for himself a new people, and it is in that action that the prophets bid Israel to place her trust (Isa. 40:28–31).

Despite the fact that it is a future act of salvation and not the past promises of God toward which the prophets direct Israel's hope, their proclamation of Yahweh's new act has the most integral relation to Israel's past traditions, for Yahweh makes it very clear through the prophets that his words to Israel in the past will also finally be fulfilled in his new act to come. Yahweh is a faithful God, and his word stands forever (Isa. 40:8). Yahweh's saving acts toward Israel in the future will therefore be modeled after his saving acts toward her in the past, and they will also serve to confirm and fulfill Yahweh's original promises to his people. Once Israel has passed through the purifying and destroying fire of the judgment—and the necessity of the judgment is emphasized in the prophetic preaching—then her new life with Yahweh will be a remarkable repetition and confirmation of the past saving histories.

For example, in her future Israel will "relive" the Hexateuchal history. God will choose Israel again (Isa. 14:1; cf. ch. 65:9), and there will be a new exodus,[36] a new wilderness wandering,[37] a new covenant,[38] a new multiplication of the population,[39] a new gift of the land,[40] a new cult with feasts and pilgrimages and sacrifices and a purified priesthood.[41] Yahweh has not forgotten his promises to the patriarchs.[42] He will keep his word, but only after Israel passes through the valley of the shadow of the judgment. Israel's rebellion against her Lord has occasioned a radical break in the salvation history. Israel does not deserve the fulfillment of the promises. Nevertheless, in his new act of salvation in the future, Yahweh will not only create Israel anew, a purified and transformed people. He will also gather up all his past words to the fathers and confirm their benefits for his people. The overflowing love and compassion of Yahweh for his own manifests itself not only in a new life but in a recovery and fulfillment for his people of all the promises from the past.

There is in most of the prophetic books, therefore, also the

70

expectation that Yahweh will keep his promise to David by setting over the new Israel a new Davidic ruler.[43] But like the promises to Israel in the Hexateuchal traditions, this promise too will find its fulfillment only in a new and transforming action on Yahweh's part. The new ruler will not be like the "shepherds" of old who had no concern for the "sheep" and who therefore were judged by Yahweh (Ezek. 34:1–10). On the other side of the destruction of the kingship, Yahweh will bring forth "a shoot from the stump of Jesse" who will be given the Spirit of Yahweh and who will thereby be enabled to rule in wisdom and obedience and righteousness and faithfulness (Isa. 11:1–5; 9:7; cf. chs. 16:5; 32:1; Jer. 23:5; 33:15). The Jeremianic traditions emphasize the humanity of the new ruler (Jer. 30:21), and certainly this is consistent with the unique Israelite understanding of the kingship, which everywhere avoids that mythological ascription of divinity to the king which was so common to the ancient Near East. Nevertheless, all the traditions emphasize the fact that the new ruler is established and enabled to rule by Yahweh alone. Micah expresses this by giving the ruler a mysterious origin: "of old, from ancient days" (Micah 5:2). In other expressions, the ruler has his strength and name from Yahweh (Micah 5:4; Jer. 23:6). He has direct access to the Lord (Jer. 30:21). He participates in Yahweh's unbreakable covenant with David (Jer. 33:17, 21). He shares in Yahweh's universal rule over the earth (Micah 5:4; Isa. 9:7; 11:10; Zech. 9:10). He comes to Israel as a man of peace, and he commands peace to all nations (Isa. 9:5, 7; Zech. 9:9–10).

Within Israel herself, then, the shepherd or prince will rule over a united people (Ezek. 37:22–24; cf. chs. 21:27; 17: 22–24), and because he has his power and ability to rule from Yahweh, he will give to Israel that security and peace and justice so longed for in the traditions of the royal psalms and here promised to Israel by the prophets in Yahweh's future salvation of her (Micah 5:4; Jer. 23:6; Isa. 32:1–7).[44]

Clearly, the fulfillment which the prophets envision of Yahweh's past promises to Israel is not to be understood as the direct working out of Yahweh's past words to his people. The fulfillment will come, according to the prophets, only by the action of a new word, which will not only create a new people with a new ruler, but which will also gather up the past words of Yahweh and bring them to completion. That is, there is rarely to be found in the Old Testament a direct line running between promise and fulfillment. Rather, the line is one of constant stops and starts, of the difficulties presented to the fulfillment by the faithlessness of Israel and the necessity of Yahweh's judgment on that faithlessness. These difficulties, this constant interaction of the word of God with Israel's response to it, occasions continual reworkings of the past traditions, continual new words interjected into Israel's life, continual new understandings of who Israel is and of how God regards her and of who she shall become. And this presents us in the Old Testament not only with a profound understanding of the necessity of Israel's suffering under judgment but also with a constant movement forward on the part of Israel and of Yahweh toward a future which only Yahweh can create and in which Israel can only hope.

Even those passages in the prophetic books which seem to envision Israel's future life simply as a return to her former state[45] nevertheless are set within the context of the radical destruction in the judgment and the radical transformation in the new age, and the return to "normalcy" turns out to be the creation within Israel of a life far more glorious than that which she has known in the past (cf. Ezek. 36:9–11, 33–36).

Israel was promised a land to call her own, according to the Hexateuchal traditions. But the land to which she will return, according to the prophets' words, will be a paradise,[46] in which Israel will enjoy absolute security (Hos. 2:18; Isa. 32:18; Zeph. 3:13; Jer. 32:37) in a covenant of peace with all creatures (Hos. 2:18; Ezek. 34:25), and a marvelous fruitfulness from nature. Indeed, the whole cosmos will be affected by Yahweh's transformation of the land, so that peace will reign in the animal world (Isa. 11:6–7; 65:25), the desert will blossom forth in watered abundance (Isa. 35:1–2, 6–7; 41:18–19), the earth will be full of the knowledge of Yahweh (Isa. 11:9; Hab. 2:14), and all nature will rejoice (Isa. 55:12–13).

In both the Hexateuchal and the monarchical traditions, Israel was promised a covenant relationship with Yahweh. That which the prophets envision in the future is Yahweh's eternal dwelling in the midst of his people[47] in an everlasting covenant of peace with them (Ezek. 37:26; Isa. 54:10). Yahweh will return to Zion[48] and make his sanctuary in the midst of his people (Ezek. 37:26) and from there reign over all the earth (Zech. 14:9; Isa. 52:7). The result is that Jerusalem with its Temple will become glorious and invincible (Isa. 54:11–17; cf. Zech., ch. 14), the bride of God (Isa. 62:4–5), protected forever (Isa. 62:6–9).[49] Its great population will need no walls (Zech. 2:4–5), for Yahweh will be its defense and its glory and light within (Isa. 60:19–20; Zech. 2:5; cf. ch. 14:7). Out of Zion will flow a river of life into all the earth (Ezek. 47:1–12; Zech. 14:8; Joel 3:18). And to Zion will come all nations for worship (Isa. 25:6; 60:7; Zech. 8:20–23; 14:16–19) and for instruction (Isa. 2:2–3). Indeed, Yahweh's return to Zion will change the very topography of the earth (cf. Isa. 40:3–5), so that Zion will become the highest mountain (Isa. 2:2), or the only one in Palestine (Zech. 14:10). And because Yahweh will reign from Zion over all the earth, peace will be established among the nations and war abolished for all time (Isa. 2:4).

The people who will enjoy the presence of God in their midst in the new life on the new Zion will be a congregation of faith, which has learned to trust Yahweh alone, which will look to him for all things (Isa. 17:7), which will accept his instruction (Isa. 29:18–19, 22–24; 30:19–22), and which will rely on him alone for deliverance, for healing, for protection.[50] This is the congregation of faith which will become the cornerstone of a new, universal people (Isa. 28:16), a congregation which will be righteous in God's eyes (Isa. 60:21; 61:3), and which can therefore serve as the "priests of the LORD" to all men and nations (Isa. 61:6).

In view of the Hexateuchal tradition that Israel would become a source of blessing for all the families of the earth, it is interesting to consider how the prophets envision the relation of the new Israel to the rest of the nations. As we have said before, there is an echo of Gen. 12:3 in the prophetic works,[51] but there is much more than that.

On the one hand, the radical change in Israel's fortunes, to be brought about by Yahweh, is pictured in terms of the service of the new Israel by other peoples. Israel's former captors will become her slaves (Isa. 14:2; 49:23; 60:14; Joel 3:4-8). They will carry Israel back to her own land (Isa. 49:22; 60:9) and rebuild her walls (Isa. 60:10), and serve her as her shepherds and plowmen and vinedressers (Isa. 61:5). All the wealth of other nations will flow into Israel (Isa. 45:14; 60:5-7, 9, 11; 61:6) and will be used in Yahweh's worship (Isa. 23:18; 60:13; Hag. 2:7-9). It is doubtful, however, that the emphasis in such pictures is on the vengeance and glorification of Israel. Rather, these promises of Israel's exaltation over the other nations are intended to show the radical nature of Yahweh's transformation of Israel's life: she who was once ruled will become the ruler; she who was once plundered and poor will become the possessor of all riches, not through her own power but through the power of Yahweh, who will be glorified in his glorification of his people.

There is therefore in the prophetic works, on the other hand, the most intimate relation between the salvation of Israel and the salvation of the rest of the world. Israel is to be saved, according to the prophets, not simply for her own sake (cf. Ezek. 20:44; 36:22-23, 32; Isa. 48:9, 11). She is to be saved as the manifestation of Yahweh's Lordship, and since Yahweh is the Lord not only of Israel but also of the world, Israel's salvation is for the purpose of bringing all nations under Yahweh's lordly rule. It is this universal divine sovereignty, this worldwide kingdom of God which the prophets finally see in their vision of the future, and Israel's redemption is the means through which the Kingdom is to come, just as in Gen. 12:1-3, Israel was to be the means through which Yahweh would bring blessing on all the earth.

The prophets picture this in various ways, although it is the

Isaiah traditions that spell it out most fully, just as it has been principally the Isaiah traditions that have dealt with Yahweh's presence on Zion and the new congregation of faith. In some passages it is simply promised that other nations, and specifically Assyria and Egypt, will come to worship Yahweh as their God (Isa. 18:7; 19:18, 19–22, 23, 24–25; cf. Zeph. 3:9; Zech. 2:11). In Isa. 56:3–8, it is promised that foreigners who keep the covenant will be accepted in the Temple, which will become a "house of prayer for all peoples." But in Deutero- and Trito-Isaiah, the means of the conversion of the nations is made clear: they will come to acknowledge that Yahweh alone is God, because they will see his Lordship and glory made manifest in his salvation of his people Israel.

Israel is Yahweh's witness to the nations in the postexilic Isaiah traditions (Isa. 43:10; 44:8; cf. chs. 55:4; 61:11; 62: 1–2), not in the sense that she sends out missionaries to other lands, but in the sense that her deliverance serves as the sign and proof to all peoples that Yahweh is Lord. When the other nations see Israel's redemption by Yahweh, they will confess:

> God is with you only, and there is no other,
> no god besides him.
>
> (Isa. 45:14; cf. v. 24; Zech. 8:23.)

They will acknowledge that God has indeed blessed Israel (Isa. 61:9; cf. Mal. 3:12), and they will therefore run to Israel (Isa. 55:5) in order to share in her light (Isa. 60:1–3; cf. ch. 66:18) and her cult (Isa. 60:6–7; 66:21, 23). In other words, the thought is that all flesh will join itself to Israel (Isa. 44:5) and "every knee shall bow," and "every tongue shall swear" (Isa. 45:23) that Yahweh alone is God and "there is no other" (Isa. 45:22).

The thought is very similar to that which is presented in a unique way in the Servant Songs of Second Isaiah. There too Israel, who is the Servant, has a mission to all the nations, but not in the sense that Israel will become a preacher or missionary (Isa. 42:1–2). Rather, Israel, the one who has been deeply despised and abhorred by the nations (Isa. 49:7; 53:3),

75

will be redeemed by Yahweh (Isa. 49:7–13); the Servant Israel, who was dead (Isa. 53:8–9, 12), will nevertheless be raised in exaltation and prosperity and triumph (Isa. 52:13 to 53:12). This salvation of Israel will then serve as a "light to the nations" (Isa. 49:6), as the way in which Yahweh enters into relation or covenant with all peoples (Isa. 49:8). When the other peoples see Israel's salvation, they will acknowledge that all the suffering and judgment that Israel has borne has been for their sake, and that by Israel's death and exaltation they have been saved (Isa. 49:6–7; 53:4–12). Yahweh's work in Israel will accomplish the salvation of all the earth. And in a unique way here the purpose of Yahweh, announced from the first in the history of the patriarchs, finds its fulfillment.

Yahweh set out in the call of Abraham to make for himself a new people, through whom he could bring blessing on all the families of the earth, in reversal of that curse under which Gen., chs. 3 to 11, saw all mankind as suffering. The prophets, and especially Deutero-Isaiah, are certain that Yahweh will accomplish his goal (cf. Isa. 40:8; 55:10–11). But for the prophets as a group, the way to Israel's salvation, and therefore to the salvation of all mankind, lies not along a path of glory, but at the end of a torturous and twisting road of suffering. Israel must undergo a judgment, in which she will be purified or die because of her sins—of that all the prophets are sure. And she will then be made new and given new life on the other side of the judgment, not for her sake, but because Yahweh is Lord and he wills to make his Lordship known to all the peoples of the earth. It is only as Yahweh is acknowledged as Lord that Israel, and through her all mankind, can know peace and wholeness and good. The earth can become "very good" again (Gen. 1:31) only under the rule of its Creator.

Chapter V

The Relation
of the Two Testaments

A. THE WORKING OF THE WORD
IN THE OLD TESTAMENT

As we have shown in the preceding chapter in connection with the prophets, the Old Testament is a history of ever-new beginnings. The prophets envision a radical break in the relationship of Israel with her God, an ending of all the old past saving assurances and the promise of a new act on Yahweh's part, which alone becomes the basis of Israel's hope and future. And yet, as we saw, the past promises of Yahweh were not cast aside by the prophets. They proclaimed that in his new act of salvation, Yahweh would gather up his previous words to Israel and bring them also to fulfillment. The new history of Yahweh with his people in the future would not only be patterned after the old history, but it would also bring the old to completion and show Yahweh to be faithful to all his words.

This pattern of breaks with the past, of new starts, of constant interruptions in the tradition histories, which nevertheless bring the total history of Yahweh's saving deeds toward his people to completion, is not confined to the prophetic literature. It is a phenomenon that characterizes the Old Testament witness to Yahweh's revelation from beginning to end.

For example, the promise of the land to the patriarchs is understood by the Deuteronomic Historian to have been fulfilled in the settlement of the twelve tribes into Canaan after the conquest under Joshua. Yet that is not the end of the matter. Even after the settlement, the gift of the land is still problematical and dependent upon Israel's willingness to love her Lord, obediently and faithfully. And the prophetic announcements that Israel will go into exile presuppose that Yahweh has reversed his promise of the land entirely for his people. Nevertheless, the promise is not left to fall into unfulfillment. Every announcement of salvation by the prophets includes a return to the land.

At the same time as this whole history of the promise of the land proceeds—and it is an extremely important one in the Old Testament's recollection—a new tradition history is begun, centering around David and Zion. The words of promise beginning this tradition history also find fulfillment, in the birth of Solomon and then in the dedication of the Temple. But that, too, is subject to recall in D's history of the sins of the kings, and once again the promise is reversed in the prophetic judgment. Yet despite the seeming failure of the promise, it is preserved and renewed in the prophetic promises of a new David and a new Zion as well as in the future hopes of both D and the Chronicler.

The promises of Yahweh, in the Old Testament's view, are fulfilled, taken away, added on to, reshaped, preserved, so that the impression left by the proclamation is one of constant interaction between Israel and a vital word of God, an interaction marked by all the details and zigzags of an ongoing and actual history. Nothing is neat here, nothing is finally formulated. Every word involves a movement forward and a constantly reassessed understanding.[1]

The result of this "dialogue" between Israel and an ever-new word of God is that the past words of Yahweh are constantly recalled and given new interpretations, not arbitrarily but in terms of Israel's new encounters with her Lord. Traditions that were once independent become fused into a new context, as happened, for example, in the fusion of the patriarchal traditions with those of Yahwism, or in the fusion of II Sam., ch. 7, with the Succession Narrative and then with D.

The introduction of older traditions into later ones reshapes the understanding of the older, which in turn exert a new influence on subsequent traditions. For example, the promise of land to Abraham certainly involved, in the patriarchal traditions, his immediate settlement into Canaan, and this was fulfilled as soon as Abraham journeyed to that distant place. But once Yahwism had appropriated the patriarchal traditions and confessed them as dealing with the actions of the God of Moses, it became apparent to both J and P that the promise of land to Abraham involved Israel as a whole, and that therefore the fulfillment of the promise was postponed until all Israel could participate in it, in the conquest under Joshua. The land became therefore, for J, in the time of Abraham, the place in which the Canaanites still lived and which they still possessed, and for P, only the place of Abraham's sojournings and his possession only in death (Gen., ch. 23). Writing from the perspective of the exile, D added his own understanding—the fulfillment under Joshua became contingent on the attitude of Israel's heart toward the Lord. Each of these understandings of the promise of the land grew out of Israel's historical encounters with her God, and no one of them can be said therefore to be "unhistorical." Rather, they mirror the fact that the word of God, in its dialogue with Israel, brought constantly new understandings and reshapings of Israel's witness to that Word.

This happened, as form criticism has shown us, not only with individual units[2] but with complexes of traditions concerning Israel's life. For example, the wilderness traditions undergo marked swings in interpretation, and the wanderings are understood both as the time of Israel's honeymoon with Yahweh (Hosea and Jeremiah), and as the time of her apostasy (Ps. 78), as the time of Yahweh's loving care for his son (Deuteronomy), and as a time of his deepest wrath (Gen., chs. 32 and 33, JE). Side by side in I Samuel stand two contradictory views of the kingship of Saul: as Yahweh's gracious response to his people's need for a king in the face of the Philistine threat (I Sam. 9:1 to 10:16; 11:27b–15), and as the people's apostasy and rejection of the kingship of Yahweh (I Sam., chs. 8;

10:17–27a; 12), a contradiction that is preserved in the prophetic views of the monarchy. It is impossible to say, furthermore, which of these views is "correct," since both must be understood as the historical result of Israel's experience with the saving institution of the monarchy. The word of God constantly creates in Israel new understandings and relationships to it, and the new never completely abrogates the old, just as the old continues to work in and through the context of the new. For this reason, the Old Testament redactors can, with no embarrassment, place seemingly totally contradictory theologies and understandings side by side in Israel's witness.

There is no doubt that interpretations are broadened and deepened in the light of Israel's experience with her God, although this process has nothing of "developmentalism" about it: that is, the new interpretation is never simply a logical development out of the old. For example, Deuteronomy's deepening of the understanding of the exodus as the supreme example of the love of God reflects not a rational deduction from the witness to the power and mercy of Yahweh in the JE stories, but the living experience of the grace of Yahweh, as it was known in seventh-century B.C. Israel through the cultic recital of Israel's history.

Israel's past with Yahweh is constantly seen in a new light by the Old Testament, because she has a present with Yahweh. And the present shapes the understanding of the past, as the past shapes the understanding of the present. Thus the prophets can base all of their preaching on the ancient demand of the First Commandment, and yet understand that commandment to apply in their situation not only to the worship of other gods but also to Israel's reliance on military weapons and foreign alliances. The ancient demand of Yahweh takes on new meaning in the light of his present demand, and yet the ancient remains and is not cast aside in favor of the new. In the same manner, the ancient Priestly tradition of the setting aside of a sabbath "rest," which is preserved for us in Genesis, can be understood in Deuteronomy as an eschatological rest promised to a faithful Israel. Or the promise to David in the royal traditions can be understood by Second Isaiah as having to do, not with a messianic figure, but with the preservation of Israel as a whole (Isa. 55:3).

Now certainly in this constant reworking of her traditions in dialogue with the present Word of God, Israel did not retain everything that was handed down to her. There were radical rejections of some material, such as the Chronicler's omission from his history of all references to the portrayals of David in I and II Samuel. Perhaps the most radical of all was Ezekiel's thoroughgoing critique of the whole of Israel's history (Ezek., chs. 20; 16; 23), in which Israel's reform movements under Hezekiah and Josiah as well as all the traditions concerning her faithfulness were ignored in favor of an interpretation of her life as one of constant uncleanness. And yet the amazing thing is that the final redactors of the Old Testament could preserve all these varying traditions and present them side by side, as legitimate and historical witnesses to Israel's encounter with the word of God.

In the light of this constant reassessment and reworking of Israel's tradition, in running dialogue with Yahweh's word, it is very difficult to speak of a unity in the Old Testament. There is no one theology to be found there, although Eichrodt is correct in saying that all presupposed Yahweh's relationship with Israel.[3] Nothing is presented outside of that relationship—not the creation stories, not the Wisdom Literature, not the secular songs—and this is exceedingly important for the interpretation of the Old Testament, as we shall see. But it is an abstraction to call that relationship, in every case, a "covenant," since that term too constantly shifts in meaning.

The major point is that nothing stands still. Because Yahweh is constantly on the move in the history of Israel, the Old Testament's witness to him constantly undergoes movement, constantly remains open toward the future that Yahweh shapes, and it is this characteristic of the Old Testament, born out of the nature of the word of God itself, which points its reader forward toward the witness of the New Testament.

B. THE WORKING OF THE WORD
IN THE NEW TESTAMENT [4]

If the Old Testament is to be considered to have an integral part in the witness to the word of God to the Christian church, if it has a legitimate place in our canon, then certainly the primary question of one preaching or teaching from the Old Testament should be, What happened to its ancient words? The entire witness of the Old Testament strains forward toward God's future, carrying forward God's ancient promises and judgments in a variety of changing testimonies. And the Old Testament ends without answering the question of whether or not God proved true, of whether or not he brought his words to completion in the history of his chosen people. The question about the fulfillment of the Old Testament is therefore nothing less than the question about God's faithfulness to his word, and finally the question of whether or not Yahweh of Israel is God.

When we move into the New Testament and seek its answers to these questions—and for the Christian who confesses that Jesus Christ is Lord, the answer can be sought in no place else —we are, however, confronted once again with a bewildering variety of testimony. As was the case in the Old Testament, we find once again that there is no one theology presented. Traditions are formulated, added on to, rejected, new materials come in to reshape the old.[5] And the impression we are given is once again of a running dialogue of the people of God with the word. Furthermore, the form criticism and tradition criticism of the New Testament—just as with Old Testament critical studies—have not reached those "assured results" which would allow us to separate all the various traditions and to place them in their proper chronology and provenance. The interpreter of the Bible therefore at times has the feeling that little can be said with finality. The living action of the word of God seems at times too dynamic to pin down in static formulations, because as soon as one statement is made, another form of the word must be taken into account. The word of God seems very often almost too lively to handle.

In dealing with the history of the action of the word of God as it is presented to us in the New Testament, therefore, we can only point to evidences of the various traditions which we have there, as they relate to the Old Testament and the question of its fulfillment. It would be very difficult to say positively in every case, for example, "This witness came first and this came second," or "This was a Hellenistic Gentile contribution, and this came from Palestinian Judaism." The New Testament, like the Old, has a way of mixing traditions all together and of not allowing its pilgrim readers to rest at any point along the journey. Although this ongoing nature of the word cannot be used as an excuse for saying nothing, it should be remembered as the background of our discussion which follows.

1. *The Witness of the New Testament to God's Inbreaking*

Judging by the witness of the Synoptic Gospels, the message of Jesus of Nazareth dealt primarily with the future coming of the Kingdom of God, understood within an apocalyptic framework. God would shortly usher in the end of the age, in judgment and salvation, through the agent of the transcendent Son of Man[6] (Mark 8:38; Luke 12:8; cf. Mark 13:26; 14:62; Matt. 10:23; Luke 17:22–37). However, Jesus apparently also understood his own words and works as the beginning of God's inbreaking, and it was in Jesus' proclamation of the Kingdom that men were confronted with its coming. (Matt. 13:16–17 and par.) His exorcisms and healings were the signs that the Kingdom had begun to come (Luke 11:20 and par.; Matt. 11:2–6), and his actions toward the sinners and the lost were the actualization of the future Kingdom in the immediate present (cf. Luke 15:1–10 and par.).

Because the future Kingdom of God was beginning to break into man's life in his own person (cf. Mark 1:14–15 and par.;

Matt. 10:7), Jesus maintained that the decision about him in the present was crucial for how a person would fare in the coming Kingdom (Mark 8:38; Luke 12:8), and the Synoptic Gospels repeatedly show us Jesus' contemporaries being confronted with such a decision.

In other words, in the Synoptic Gospels we have the witness to the fact that God has once again begun a new action in the history of Israel. As Yahweh broke into history in the time of Abraham and David and the prophets, so once again he breaks into Israel's history in the ministry of Jesus of Nazareth. But the testimony of the Synoptics is that this is the final, decisive inbreaking; this is the intervention that has significance for the Kingdom; this is the interruption that leads to the determination of how one will stand at the end. That final day toward which the Old Testament strained has now begun to come.

Such apparently were the initial data with which the followers of Jesus had to deal. In the proclamation and activity of Jesus of Nazareth they were confronted with the immediate presence and saving activity of God, and that confrontation placed them before the final life or death decision.

Then came the horror and disillusionment of the crucifixion, which apparently cast doubt on all the followers' experiences with Jesus and called into question the conviction that God had confronted them through him. But their doubt was changed into faith and joy in the experience of the resurrection, and all that they had sensed in the presence of Jesus was confirmed and enlightened. He was indeed the one in whom the Kingdom of God had begun to break in. He was in truth the one through whom God was present and working. He was indubitably the focus of all decision, and whether or not one believed in him determined one's life or death. The followers of Jesus therefore set out to proclaim who Jesus was, in order to bring men to a decision about him, and in order to call men to trust in him as the way to life. As Reginald Fuller has put it, "the Proclaimer became the Proclaimed," [7] and these efforts of the followers of Jesus to tell who he was form the basis of the New Testament's Christological witness.

84

2. *The Kerygma of the Resurrection*

It has been held [8] that the earliest Christology of the primitive Palestine Christian community centered about the proclamation of Jesus as the Son of Man. That is, Jesus' own message had been vindicated by the resurrection. He was in fact the one in whom the Kingdom of God had begun to come. Thus, the Son of Man was not a figure separate from Jesus of Nazareth, but he himself was, in his earthly ministry, already the "proleptic" Son of Man, and he himself was the one who would come in judgment and salvation as the transcendent Son of Man at the end of the age.

Certainly the evidence of Q and Mark points to the fact that very early the Palestinian church transformed the Son of Man sayings to set forth this kerygma. Because of his resurrection, Jesus was in heaven and would come soon as the Son of Man. To picture this coming, the Old Testament tradition, not only of Dan. 7:13 (in Mark 13:26), but also of Ps. 110:1 (in Mark 14:62), was called upon. However, Jesus was not only the Son of Man who was to come; he was also in his earthly ministry already the Son of Man (Matt. 8:20 and par.; 11:19 and par.; Mark 2:10, 28). This meant, then, that he was the suffering Son of Man, who was rejected by men and delivered into the hands of sinners (Mark 14:41 and par.), in fulfillment of the Scriptures (Mark 14:21 and par.), but who was vindicated by God then in his resurrection (Mark 8:31 and par.; 9:31 and par.; 10:32–34 and par.).

It seems inconceivable, however, that the fact of the resurrection itself did not form the *center* of the earliest kerygma of the church. Certainly in one of the oldest traditions in the New Testament (I Cor. 15:3–5), the resurrection, along with the death, forms the heart of the proclamation. And it is evident in Mark that the community's early recounting of the suffering of the Son of Man included the promise of his resurrection (Mark 8:31; 9:31; 10:32–34). Did not the early Christian communities, at the same time that they proclaimed Jesus to be the

Son of Man, both in his earthly ministry and at the end of the age to come, also emphasize the fact of his resurrection?

To answer this question, it is necessary to isolate the language of the resurrection, and to show what terms the early communities used to express the fact that Jesus had been raised. As this is done, it begins to become clear just who the early Christian communities believed Jesus of Nazareth to be.

Primary to the proclamation of the resurrection was the assertion that Jesus had been raised to the right hand of God. This is found in the Marcan Son of Man saying in Mark 14:62; in the apparently early tradition of Stephen's death in Acts 7:55, where Jesus is once again identified with the Son of Man; in Paul's letter to the Romans (Rom. 8:34); and in the speeches of Peter in Acts 2:32–33 and 5:30–31. In short, it seems clear that some of the earliest language used to describe the resurrection in both Palestinian and Hellenistic communities was the language of the exaltation to the right hand of God, which was borrowed from the royal Psalm 110 (v. 1) in the Old Testament. And it is clear from Eph. 1:20; Col. 3:1; Heb. 1:3; 8:1; 10:12; 12:2; and I Peter 3:22 that this language persisted into the later theologies of the New Testament churches. The risen Jesus was, therefore, described not only as the Son of Man but also as a royal figure exalted to the right hand of God to share in God's power and rule.[9]

This was by no means the only motif of the royal theology of Ps. 110 applied to the risen Jesus, however. In both fairly early (I Cor. 15:25–28) and later passages (Eph. 1:22), as well as in Hebrews (ch. 10:13) and I Peter (ch. 3:22), the thought of Ps. 110:1 that God would put all the ruler's enemies under his feet is given expression, although the subjection remains a future event in I Corinthians and Hebrews, while it is thought of as an already accomplished fact in the other passages.

That which was emphasized by these uses of Ps. 110 was the fact that the exalted Jesus had been made Lord (cf. Acts 2:34–36), and it has now been agreed among most New Testament scholars[10] that the ancient liturgical formula preserved for us in I Cor. 16:22, *Marana tha,* "Our Lord, come!" represents one of the earliest invocations used by the Palestinian Christian communities, just as the confession, "Jesus is Lord," contained in the traditional material of Rom. 10:9, represents one of the earliest credos. Jesus, by being exalted to the right hand of God by his resurrection, had become Lord, and it was primarily as the Lord that his followers not only invoked his name in worship and prayer (cf. Rom. 10:13; Acts 7:59) but also awaited his coming (Matt. 7:21 and par.; Luke 13:25). Thus, in the ancient Christological hymn of Phil., ch. 2, the thought is that "God has highly exalted him" (Phil. 2:9), i.e., God has raised him from the dead and, by implication, placed him on his right hand, and "bestowed on him the name which is above every name" (Phil. 2:9), that is, "Lord" (Phil. 2:11). In the much later passage of Ephesians this whole cluster of testimonies—resurrection, exaltation to the right hand, rule over enemies, Lordship—rising out of the use of Ps. 110, appears as a unity:

> . . . which he accomplished in Christ when he raised him from the dead and made him sit at his right hand in the heavenly places, far above all rule and authority and power and dominion, and above every name that is named, not only in this age but also in that which is to come; and he has put all things under his feet. (Eph. 1:20–22.)

It was, to summarize, in the language of the royal theology of the Old Testament, represented by Ps. 110, that both early and later Christian communities, both Jewish and Hellenistic, proclaimed the resurrection/exaltation of Jesus and his resulting Lordship.[11] Perhaps this language was used because Jesus himself used Ps. 110 to refer to the Christ (Mark 12:35–37a and par.).[12] At any rate, the language of the psalm was used to give expression to the heart of the Christian kerygma—that Jesus of Nazareth had been raised from the dead and now was Lord, at the right hand of God.

3. The Kerygma of the Earthly Ministry

The use of the language from the royal theology of the Old Testament carried with it the implication that Jesus was the one to whom the Old Testament royal traditions looked forward, and thus, in the light of the resurrection, the earthly ministry of Jesus also was illumined as the fulfillment of the Old Testament hopes surrounding the kingship.

a. Jesus as the Messiah

Reginald Fuller is probably correct in stating that the earliest designations of Jesus as the Messiah looked forward to his *parousia* as the coming Son of Man/Messiah,[13] since both Peter's confession in Mark 8:29, and the attribution to Jesus of Messiahship in Mark 14:62 and par. are connected with the future coming of the Son of Man.[14] There is no other early evidence to show either that Jesus thought of himself as the Messiah during his earthly ministry or that his followers called him by that name. The triumphal entry into Jerusalem in Mark celebrates only "the kingdom of our father David that is coming" (Mark 11:10); the baptism and transfiguration narratives (Mark 1:9–11; 9:2–8) do not use the term. The accounts of the trial before Pilate and of the crucifixion in Mark, ch. 15 and par., make it clear that Jesus was crucified as a messianic pretender, but the implication may be that the charge was a false one. As we shall see, it is not the title "Messiah" which Mark gives to Jesus, but another royal designation, "Son of God."

Matthew enlarges significantly on the designation of Jesus as the Messiah only in the narrative of the Wise Men (Matt. 2:2, 4–6) and in the story concerning the Baptist (Matt. 11:2). Luke includes the title in the birth and infancy narratives (Luke 2:11, 26), but he places it in Jesus' mouth only after the resurrection (Luke 24:46), although Luke 4:41 states that the demons knew that Jesus "was the Christ." This is in line with what we find in Acts, in which Jesus is the Christ (Acts 9:22; 17:3; 18:5, 28; 26:23) and yet he is appointed such only after the resurrection (Acts 2:36; 3:18–21). In short, the Synoptic writers do not emphasize the Messiahship of Jesus on earth.

In the continual task of proclaiming who Jesus was, as that proclamation was acted upon and reinterpreted in the light of the experience of the risen Christ's presence in the church (the ongoing encounter with the Word of God), the followers of Jesus nevertheless came to the conviction that Jesus had been the Messiah during his earthly ministry, and in the Fourth Gospel we find a thoroughgoing messianism connected with Jesus' life. Thus, Andrew tells his brother, Simon Peter, "We have found the Messiah" (John 1:41). Jesus is made to claim the title in his conversation with the woman of Samaria (John 4:24–26). And Martha, the sister of Lazarus, confesses her faith in the Messiahship of Jesus in a passage which some have connected with the catechetical instruction of the church (John 11:27). Similarly, there is a running motif throughout the first twelve chapters of the Gospel, which pictures the questioning of the people; those who hear and see Jesus are repeatedly portrayed as asking:

Can this be the Christ? (John 4:29.)

Can it be that the authorities really know that this is the Christ? (John 7:26.)

Is the Christ to come from Galilee? (John 7:41.)

If you are the Christ, tell us plainly. (John 10:24; cf. ch. 9:22.)

We have heard from the law that the Christ remains for ever. How can you say that the Son of man must be lifted up? Who is this Son of man? (John 12:34.)

As if in answer to this questioning and disbelief of the multitudes, the Gospel writer concludes his work, "These are written that you may believe that Jesus is the Christ." (John 20:31.) When we come to I John, then, the belief in the messiahship of Jesus has become an article of faith: "Every one who believes that Jesus is the Christ is a child of God." (I John 5:1.)

To say that John's views of Jesus as the Messiah during his

earthly ministry are "incorrect" or "unhistorical" is to ignore the way the word of God works in the growth of the Biblical tradition. The Gospel According to John is as much a product of the confrontation with the risen Lord as are the Synoptics, and both the Fourth Gospel and the Synoptics are confessions of faith rising out of that confrontation. But the Fourth Gospel's confession of Jesus as the earthly Messiah furnishes a vivid example of the continual reinterpretation given to the tradition in the light of the ongoing working of the Word among the various congregations of the people of God.

b. Jesus as the Son of David

In Jewish messianology, the coming Messiah was to be a descendant of David, and the sources also record the belief that Jesus was descended from that royal line. Paul knows the tradition of Jesus' Davidic descent (Rom. 1:3), Mark 10:47 f. states it, and Mark 11:10 implies it, an implication which is then made explicit in Matt. 21:9. The record of Jesus' dispute with the scribes in Mark 12:35–37 and par. does deny that the Christ is the Son of David, but certainly the attribution to Jesus of Davidic lineage by Matthew (Matt. 1:1) and Luke (Luke 1:32, 69; 2:11; 3:31; Acts 2:30) seems in accord with most early tradition. Matthew and Luke trace Jesus' descent from David through the line of Joseph (Matt. 1:6–16; Luke 3:23–31), despite the fact that such genealogies contradict their stories of the miraculous conception of Jesus by the Holy Spirit.[15]

The Fourth Gospel also implies that it knows the tradition of Jesus' birth at Bethlehem, "the village where David was" (John 7:42), but this is the only mention in John of Jesus' Davidic line, a surprising fact in view of John's emphasis on Jesus' messiahship. Apparently in the view of the writer of John, Jesus' Davidic descent contributed little to the proof of his messiahship. By the time we get to Revelation, however, we find an emphatic affirmation of Jesus' Davidic line and his messiahship (Rev. 5:5; 22:16), and in II Tim. 2:8, we have evidence that Jesus' Davidic descent was an established part of the early preaching of some churches.

The traditions concerning the Davidic descent of the Messiah rested principally on the promise to David in II Sam., ch. 7, and it is to that promise that Acts 2:30 points in connection with Jesus (cf. Heb. 1:5b). Jesus was the heir of David who had ascended to his father's throne; Jesus was the Messiah therefore who was to come. In Revelation, on the other hand, it is Gen. 49:9 and Num. 24:17 which are used to speak of Jesus' Davidic descent. Both are passages that were originally applied simply to David and his line, but that took on a messianic interpretation in subsequent development.[16] But it is once again in the language of the Old Testament that the New Testament traditions proclaim who Jesus was.

c. Jesus as the Son of God

The Q tradition in Matt. 11:25–27 and par. points to what may have been Jesus' own sense of a unique relationship with the Father. But certainly the application of the title "Son of God" to Jesus was the result of the church's attempt to proclaim who he was, and once again we find at least major portions of that proclamation resting on the language of the Old Testament.[17]

It is not Ps. 110 or II Sam., ch. 7, that is quoted in relation to Jesus' Sonship, despite the fact that II Sam. 7:14 promised that the heir of David would be the adopted Son of God—a fact that Heb. 1:5b does indeed recall. Rather, it is the royal Psalm 2 that is used most often in the New Testament to portray Jesus as the Son of God, and we see in the use of Ps. 2 the increasing expansion of the kerygma within the framework of the Old Testament royal theology. Apparently at the time of Jesus, the title "Son of God" had only just begun to be used in relation to the Messiah in Palestinian Judaism, but it had been used in Hellenistic Judaism as a title for the righteous man (cf. Wisd. of Sol. 2:16–18; 5:5), and apparently it was in a Hellenistic Jewish–Christian environment that the term developed its meaning in relation to Jesus.[18]

It is this royal term, and not "Messiah," which Mark prefers to use of Jesus. Thus, at the baptism, the voice from heaven declares, "Thou art my beloved Son; with thee I am well pleased," in the language of Ps. 2:7 and Isa. 42:1 (Mark 1:11 and par.), and this sonship is then confirmed in the transfiguration revelation (Mark 9:2–8 and par.), where the words of Ps. 2:7 and Deut. 18:15 (?) are used. (The parallel in Matt. 17:5 retains also the reference to Isa. 42:1.) The use of "Son of God" in Mark, however, points largely toward the exalted Jesus, an exaltation which is prefigured at the baptism, confirmed in the transfiguration (cf. II Peter 1:17), and begun at the crucifixion. Thus, the centurion at the foot of the cross, upon seeing that Jesus has died, confesses, "Truly this man was the Son of God!" (Mark 15:39 and par.; incorrectly translated in RSV footnote). Similarly, in the trial before the high priest, Jesus is the "Son of the Blessed" who is identified with the "Christ" and the coming "Son of man" (Mark 14:61–62 and par.).

Further, there are only the most tentative leanings in Matthew and Luke toward the extension of the term to cover Jesus' earthly life. In Acts 13:33, the use of Ps. 2:7 is still in reference to the risen Jesus (cf. Acts 9:20). But the parable of Mark 12:1–11 and par. had suggested that Jesus was already Son of God on earth, and Matthew's account of Peter's confession makes Peter confirm this fact (Matt. 16:16). Luke puts it differently. In Luke 1:32, the angel promises Mary that Jesus will be called "the Son of the Most High," but then it is the supernatural figures alone who know that Jesus is the Son of God—the demons (Luke 4:41) and the devil (Luke 4:3, 9 and par.), a motif that had been present already in Mark's story of the Gerasene demoniac (Mark 5:1–20, v. 7 and par.).

As for the conception of Jesus as the Son of God on earth because of the virgin birth (Matt. 1:18–25; Luke 1:26–38), a different set of traditions come into play. The virginity of Mary is based on Isa. 7:14 in the LXX, and the concept clashes in Matthew and Luke with the tradition of the Davidic descent of Jesus, which forms the context of it. Thus, Fuller has seen the concept of the virgin birth as a product of Hellenistic Jewish

Christianity and as a modified expression of the Hellenistic Jewish concept of divine man.[19]

We see the expansion of the kerygma once again in the Gospel of John, where Jesus is clearly the Son of God on earth (John 1:14, 34) and is openly so confessed (John 1:49; 11:27). Further, the term is repeatedly linked with that of "Messiah" (John 1:49; 11:27), so that these two concepts from the royal theology become merged, and the writer concludes his Gospel, "These are written that you may believe that Jesus is the Christ, the Son of God" (John 20:31). In the same manner, I John links the concepts of "Messiah" and "Son of God" (I John 5:1, 5). The Son of God has appeared on earth "to destroy the works of the devil" (I John 3:8), and the confession that Jesus is the Son of God has been made an article of faith (I John 4:15; cf. ch. 5:10–13).

The end result in the traditions is that both Ps. 110 and Ps. 2 from the royal theology of the Old Testament have been called into play to express who Jesus was, along with Isa. 42:1 and perhaps Deut. 18:15, which we shall subsequently discuss.

d. Jesus as the Shepherd

One other point should be made in connection with the use of royal motifs in dealing with Jesus' earthly ministry. In the Old Testament, both Yahweh[20] and kings or leaders or princes[21] of Israel or of the foreign nations are called "shepherds" of their people. And in Ezek. 34:23 and 37:24, the Davidic prince who is to come is specifically given this title.

Mark only hints at the royal motifs connected with the conception of Jesus as the shepherd of his people. Mark 6:34 and par. applies I Kings 22:17 (cf. Num. 27:17) to Jesus as the prelude to the feeding of the five thousand, and Mark 14:27 applies the prophecy of Zech. 13:7 to the falling away of Jesus' disciples at the time of the crucifixion. Both I Kings 22:17 and Zech. 13:7 use "shepherd" to refer to royal figures. But John, ch. 10, is much more specific. Jesus is the good shepherd. Unlike the shepherds who came before him who scattered the flock and fed only themselves (Jer. 23:1 ff.; Ezek. 34:2 ff.; John 10:8), Jesus is the one who cares for his sheep (cf. Jer. 23:4), who gives them abundant life (cf. Ezek. 34:11–16; John 10:10), who will gather all together in one flock under one shepherd (John 10:16), as promised in Ezek. 34:23 and ch. 37:24 (cf. Isa. 56:8). It seems apparent that John is here casting Jesus in the role of the shepherd-prince David, promised by the prophet.

By the time of Hebrews and I Peter, the reference to Jesus as the Shepherd therefore seems to have become one of the standard liturgical formulas used of Jesus in the church (cf. Heb. 13:20; I Peter 2:25).

e. Jesus as the Mosaic Prophet-Servant

We have seen in Mark's accounts of the baptism and transfiguration that not only Ps. 2:7 was called into play to tell who Jesus was but also Isa. 42:1 and perhaps Deut. 18:15. That is, in addition to the use of the royal ideology of Ps. 2, there is also the application to Jesus of one of the Servant Songs of Second Isaiah and perhaps of the Deuteronomic promise of a prophet like Moses. Certainly the use of these three strands of Old Testament tradition is found not only in Mark but also with some variations in some of the speeches in Acts.[22]

Without trying to disentangle or to put into chronological order these various strands of tradition, let us merely point to the evidence regarding Jesus' identification with Moses, with the prophet, and with the servant.

There is some suggestion that Mark's accounts of the temptation and of the feeding of the five thousand have been influenced by the Old Testament picture of Moses. The "forty days" of the temptation (Mark 1:13) are reminiscent of Moses' forty days and forty nights on Mt. Sinai (Ex. 34:28; Deut. 9:9, 18), and the feeding is placed in "a lonely place" (Mark 6:35), suggestive of the desert and the giving of the manna. Whether Mark had the figure of Moses in mind or not can only be conjectured however.

But certainly John, ch. 6, connects the feeding of the five thousand with the giving of the manna, and The Gospel According to Matthew seems deliberately to present Jesus as a new Moses, drawing several parallels between Jesus' activity and that of the Old Testament figure. For example, just as the Pharaoh of Egypt tried to do away with all the Hebrew male infants (Ex. 1:15–22), so Herod tries to do away with the infant Jesus by slaughtering all the male children under two years of age in the region of Bethlehem (Matt. 2:16–18). Just as Moses gave the covenant commandments to the old Israel on the mount of Sinai, so Jesus gives the new commandments to his disciples on the new mount (Matt., chs. 5 to 7 [23]), and these are contrasted with commandments in the law of Moses (Matt. 5:21, 27, 31, 33, 38). Just as Moses took Aaron, Nadab, and Abihu with him when he went up Mt. Sinai (Ex. 24:1, 9), so Jesus takes Peter, James, and John with him up the Mount of Transfiguration (Matt. 17:1 and par.). But whereas Moses' face shone with reflected glory from talking with God in his glory on Mt. Sinai (Ex. 34:29), Jesus' face shines with his own glory (Matt. 17:2 [24]). As the divine voice was heard at Sinai (cf. Deut. 5:22–26), so it is heard once again on the Mount of Transfiguration (Matt. 17:5–6 and par.).

In Acts we find a different conception of Jesus' connection with Moses, however. According to Deut. 18:15, Moses had promised Israel, "The LORD your God will raise up for you a prophet like me from among you, from your brethren—him you shall heed." Probably every individual prophet in Israel during the classical age of prophecy was understood as the fulfillment of this Mosaic promise. But in the postexilic period, this promise took on eschatological dimensions, and there arose the expectation of a special prophet who would accompany the coming of kingly and priestly Messiahs, as can be seen in the Dead Sea Scrolls.[25] By the time of Jesus, this expectation had become a part of popular Palestinian hopes, as evidenced in the Fourth Gospel (John 1:21, 25; 6:14; 7:40). In Acts, then, Jesus is specifically identified with this eschatological prophet who was to come (Acts 3:22–26), and as such is also called "the Holy and Righteous One" and "the Author of life" (Acts 3:14–15). In Acts 7:37, the promise of Moses in Deut. 18:15 is quoted and in Acts 7:52, Jesus is once again "the Righteous One," i.e., the eschatological prophet. We have also suggested that the phrase "listen to him," in Mark's account of the transfiguration (Mark 9:7), is a reference to "him you shall heed" from Deut. 18:15, but we will not push this. Jesus is, at any rate, understood as the eschatological prophet, fulfilling the promise of Moses, in the Christology of Acts, chs. 3 and 7.

As we noted earlier, alongside these references to Jesus as the Mosaic prophet, there is in Acts, ch. 3, and Acts 4:24–30 also the reference to Jesus as "servant." We therefore have to ask first where this combining of Moses-prophet-servant traditions came from, and second, why it was used in Acts to tell who Jesus was.

Certainly Moses is called the "servant" of the Lord in the Old Testament, not only in the sense of being one of those who submits himself to God's commands (Ex. 4:10; Num. 11:11; Deut. 3:24) but also in the sense of being a special instrument of God's working (Ex. 14:31; Num. 12:7 f.). This latter is especially pronounced in Deuteronomy (Deut. 34:5) and Joshua (Josh. 1:1; 8:31; 11:12; 12:6; 13:8; etc.) where the phrase "Moses the servant of the LORD" has become a standardized descriptive formula.

Moreover, Moses is clearly a prophet in the J, E, and D sources of the Old Testament. Indeed, he is a prophet above all other prophets (Num. 12:7–8; Deut. 34:10), and as such is the mediator of the covenant commandments to Israel (Deut. 5:22 ff.). And in the New Testament, there is evidence that Jesus was considered by some of the people to be a prophet (cf. Mark 6:15 and par.; 8:28 and par.; Matt. 21:11, 46; Luke 24:19), and perhaps even so considered himself (Mark 6:4 and par.; Luke 13:33). In addition, Jesus' suffering death was early connected with that of the Suffering Servant of Isa., ch. 53, as we shall see.

But the above facts about Moses do not make it fully clear

why Jesus was identified with him, and this can be explicated only if the full picture of Moses in the Old Testament is seen. In his role as a prophet above all other prophets, Moses is made the model and type of a prophet, as is clear in Num. 12:7–8 and is implied in the promise of Deut. 18:15. As such a prophet, Moses fulfills the prophetic function of being an intercessor before God for his sinful people (Ex. 32:31 f.; Num. 14:13–19; cf. Amos 7:1–6; Jer. 7:16). But as an intercessor, Moses becomes a suffering mediator between God and the people. In Ex. 32:32, Moses is willing to become anathema in order to save Israel, and in D, Moses is repeatedly pictured in his suffering role. When he goes up the mountain to receive the Ten Commandments, he undergoes the asceticism of forty days and forty nights without food and water (Deut. 9:9; cf. Ex. 34:28). After the incident of the golden calf, he again undergoes such stringent asceticism, pleading that the Lord not destroy his sinful people (Deut. 9:18–20; cf. vs. 25–29). And he finally dies outside the Promised Land, bearing the sins of his people in himself, that Israel may enter into the land promised to the fathers (Deut. 1:37; 3:23–27; 4:21–22).[26]

It has further been suggested by von Rad [27] and others[28] that the Suffering Servant of Deutero-Isaiah is intended to be a picture of the prophet like Moses, who was to come (Deut. 18:15). Without going into detail, we mention this idea, since there are many correspondences between the figure of Moses and the Suffering Servant, although it interprets the Suffering Servant in terms different from those which we have suggested in the previous chapter. But since Jesus' death was early understood in terms of Isa., ch. 53 (see below), it would be easy to see why the Mosaic prophet-servant traditions were used to describe who Jesus was. The eschatological prophet like Moses was the Suffering Servant, who in turn was Jesus of Nazareth.

It is interesting in this connection that the two traditions of Jesus' use of the term "prophet" to describe himself relate to his suffering and death (Mark 6:4 and par.; Luke 13:33), and that the Q saying of Matt. 23:37–39 and par. (cf. vs. 29–30 and

97

par.) seems to represent Jesus' mission as the final prophetic message to Israel, which is rejected at his death. In short, in those traditions in which Jesus sees himself as a prophet, his prophetic role is connected with suffering.

f. Jesus as the Servant

There are a few passages, however, in Luke and in Matthew, which connect Jesus' activities during his lifetime with the Servant of Second Isaiah, and yet they have nothing to do with the conception in Acts of Jesus as the Mosaic prophet-servant to come. In Luke 2:32, the aged Simeon quotes Isa. 42:6 in his blessing of the infant Jesus: Jesus is to be God's "light for revelation to the Gentiles, and for glory to thy people Israel." In Matt. 12:18–21, Jesus' admonitions to those whom he has healed that they should not make him known are understood as the fulfillment of Isa. 42:1–4, while in Matt. 8:17, Jesus' healing ministry is understood as the fulfillment of Isa. 53:4. Similarly, the Gospel of John (John 12:38) understands the disbelief of the Jews as the fulfillment of Isa. 53:1. In all these passages, the figure of the Servant in Second Isaiah is used as the explanation of who Jesus is,[29] and if Isa., chs. 35 and 61, belong also with Second Isaiah, as some scholars think they do, Jesus is made to identify himself with the Servant in the Q saying of Matt. 11:4–5 and par., which quotes from Isa. 35:5–6 and 61:1 as well as from Isa. 29:18–19.

It should further be noted that in the Synoptics and in Acts, Jesus is given the Spirit at his baptism (Mark 1:11 and par.), as the Servant of Isa. 42:1 and 61:1 is given it, and that Jesus then is the possessor of the Spirit (cf. Matthew's transformation of the Q saying, Matt. 12:28; the use of Isa., ch. 61, in Luke 4:16 ff.; and Acts 10:38).

Paul of course says very little about the earthly life of Jesus, and it is the preaching of Christ to the Gentiles which he sees as the confirmation of Isa. 52:15 (Rom. 15:21), just as the preaching of the gospel to all men is the realization of Isa. 52:7, according to Rom. 10:15, and the disbelief of the Jews the confirmation of Isa. 53:1, according to Rom. 10:16. Thus, it is the risen and preached Christ whom Paul relates to the Servant.

In working with the Old Testament tradition of the Servant, Paul further introduces into the tradition a unique reinterpretation. As we saw in the previous chapter, the viewpoint of Second Isaiah is that the salvation of Israel will lead the Gentiles to acknowledge that God is with Israel only (Isa. 45:14; 52:13–15), so that they too will come into Israel (Isa. 44:5) and worship Yahweh and confess that the transformed Israel, the Suffering Servant, has suffered on their account and borne their iniquities (Isa. 53:4–6). It is through the suffering and subsequent exaltation and salvation of Israel that the Gentiles will be saved. In Paul's thought in Romans, this viewpoint is exactly reversed. It is through the salvation of the Gentiles in Christ that Israel will be saved. According to Rom., ch. 11, when the Jews see the salvation of the Gentiles, they will become jealous (Rom. 11:11, 14) and thus come to acknowledge that it is through faith in Christ alone that they may receive mercy from God (Rom. 11:31). The church has replaced Israel in Paul's conception—a viewpoint that we shall later discuss at length—and Second Isaiah's vision of the Suffering Servant has found its realization in Christ, whom the church proclaims to all men.

4. *The Kerygma of the Crucifixion*

Certainly one of the earliest parts of the witness to Jesus was the proclamation of the saving significance of his death. This proclamation existed from the first alongside that of the resurrection, as is evidenced in the traditional material of I Cor. 15:3 and in the sayings concerning the suffering of the Son of Man (Mark 8:31 and par.; 9:12 and par.; 9:31 and par.; 10:33 and par.; 14:21 and par.; cf. Luke 17:25; 24:7). Moreover, integral to this proclamation was the statement that Christ died for our sins "in accordance with the scriptures" (I Cor. 15:3; cf. Mark 9:12; 14:21, 49), which connected the death of Jesus with the witness of the Old Testament. The tradition once again turned to the Book of the Old Covenant to tell who Jesus was and what he did, and the saving significance of his death was seen within the framework of several different tradition complexes of the Hebrew scriptures.

a. Jesus' Death and the Suffering Servant

One of the earliest interpretations of the crucifixion was that which compared and indeed identified Jesus' death with the death of the Suffering Servant as seen in Second Isaiah's vision, Isa. 52:13 to 53:12. In fact, it may have been this initial identification of Jesus' death with that of the Servant which led to the interpretation of Jesus as the Servant in his earthly ministry, as discussed above.

It is now widely agreed among scholars[30] that the saying of Mark 10:45b is based upon Isa., ch. 53: "The Son of man . . . came . . . to give his life as a ransom for many," the latter part of which is a reference to Isa. 53:10–12. In the same manner, Mark 14:24b; Rom. 5:18; and Rom. 4:25 (which may be early pre-Pauline traditional material) all see Jesus' death in terms of the vicarious suffering for sin of the Deutero-Isaianic Servant (cf. Gal. 1:4). This usage continues then into the traditions of Hebrews (Heb. 9:28) and I Timothy (I Tim. 2:6).

This identification of Jesus with the Servant of Isa., ch. 53, is also quite pervasive throughout the various portrayals of the passion. Jesus is the one who is silent before his oppressors (Isa. 53:7; cf. Mark 14:61 and par.; 15:5 and par.; Luke 23:9; John 19:9), who is reckoned with transgressors (Isa. 53:12, which is quoted in Luke 22:37), who is like a lamb led to the slaughter (Isa. 53:7, which is quoted in Acts 8:32), who is the Lamb of God that takes away the sins of the world (Isa. 53:7; John 1:29, cf. v. 36), whose grave is made with a rich man (Isa. 53:9; Matt. 27:57–60), and yet who had committed no sin and spoken no guile (Isa. 53:9; I Peter 2:22). Jesus is the one by whose stripes we were healed when we had gone astray like sheep (Isa. 53:5–6; I Peter 2:24–25). In all these passages, the writers understood Jesus as the Suffering Servant promised by Second Isaiah.

Further, while The Gospel According to John does not use as many references to Isa., ch. 53, in its passion story as do the Synoptics, the comparisons between John's view of the crucifixion and the exaltation of the Servant are striking. In John, Jesus' crucifixion is made the moment of his exaltation before the world (John 3:14; 8:28; 12:34). It is when Jesus is lifted up that he will draw all men to himself (John 12:32), just as the exaltation of the Servant in Isa. 52:13 to 53:12 will bring all nations into Israel. Just as Israel, the Servant, will serve as a light to the nations in Isa. 42:6 and 49:6, so Jesus is, in John 12:30–36 (cf. John 12:38 where Isa. 53:1 is quoted), the light in the world. And just as the salvation of Israel, the Servant, will be her glorification and the glorification of God according to Second Isaiah (Isa. 43:7; 45:25; 55:5; cf. chs. 40:5; 41:16; 42:8; 44:23; 46:13; 48:11; 49:3), so the death of Jesus on the cross is his glorification and the glorification of the Father (John 13:31 f.; 17:1). It seems possible that John was deliberately drawing a parallel in these passages between Jesus and the Servant of Second Isaiah.

b. Jesus' Death and the Exodus-Redemption Traditions

The interpretation of the passion in terms of the Suffering Servant is by no means the only view of the crucifixion in the New Testament. There is also in the very early traditions the understanding of the crucifixion in terms of the exodus and redeemer traditions of the Old Testament, and this is especially true in Paul's writings.

Despite the fact that Paul is an apostle to the Gentile world, he draws heavily on the Old Testament's view of the exodus to explain the significance of Christ's death. Central to the Old Testament's view is the tradition that Yahweh's deliverance of his people Israel out of Egypt was his "redemption" of them.[31] Thus in Second Isaiah, Yahweh is repeatedly named the "Redeemer" of Israel [32] because in the second exodus which the prophet envisions, Yahweh will once again redeem his people,[33] as he did in the original deliverance from Egypt.

The concept of "redemption" has a very specific content in the Old Testament, however. A "redeemer" in secular usage in Israel was one who bought back a piece of family property that had fallen to someone outside of the family (Lev. 25:25–34; cf. Jer. 32:6–15), or it was one who bought back a relative who had become a slave (cf. Ex. 21:8; Lev. 25:47–55). When the Children of Israel confessed Yahweh to be their "Redeemer" from Egypt, they were therefore saying that Yahweh was the relative who bought them back from slavery in Egypt. Specifically, Yahweh was the Father of Israel, and from the time of the exodus onward, Israel was his son (Hos. 11:1; Ex. 4:22; Jer. 31:20; Isa. 63:16).

It is against the background of this exodus-redemption tradition that Paul writes, "You were bought with a price" (I Cor. 6:20; 7:23) and urges the Corinthians not to fall again into slavery to men (I Cor. 7:23). The death of Christ on the cross is the redemption price which God has paid to buy the Christian from slavery. Perhaps the reference to God's passing over former sins, in Rom. 3:25, is a reference to the Passover at the time of the exodus. But certainly the exodus is recalled in I Cor. 5:7, "Christ, our paschal lamb, has been sacrificed." In Galatians, the redemption wrought by the death of Christ is related to freeing the Christian from slavery to the law: "Christ redeemed us from the curse of the law" (Gal. 3:13), and the purpose of this redemption, then, is "that we might receive adoption as sons" (Gal. 4:5), exactly as Israel was made the son of God at the exodus, so that we too may cry, "Abba! Father!" to God (Gal. 4:6). We are no longer slaves, but sons, and if sons, then heirs to all the promises to Israel (Gal. 3:29; cf. Col. 1:13–14). It is from the richness of the Old Testament's view of the exodus redemption that Paul interprets the significance of the death of Christ on the cross.

This relating of the crucifixion to the redemption of the

exodus with its Passover is inherent also in the Johannine account of the crucifixion, in which Christ's death is placed on the day of Passover and thus equated with the slaying of the Paschal lamb (John 19:14, 31).

c. Jesus' Death and the Sinai Traditions

Based on the early tradition of the Last Supper, which Paul preserves in I Cor. 11:23–26 (cf. Mark 14:12–25 and par.), there is also the interpretation of Jesus' death from the standpoint of the Sinai covenant, and this is often combined with the exodus-Passover tradition. In both Paul and the Synoptics, the cup at the Last Supper represents the blood of the new covenant (I Cor. 11:25; Mark 14:24 and par.; cf. I Cor. 10:16), and in Heb. 8:5–6; 9:18–20; 12:18–24; and Rev. 5:9–10 the context of this tradition is clearly the cutting of the covenant on Mt. Sinai by Moses. However, in both Heb. 9:15 and Rev. 1:5–6; 5:9, this covenant tradition is connected with the "redemption" or "ransom" of Israel from Egypt, and thus Christ's death becomes connected with the whole of the exodus-Sinai act of God. Indeed, John, ch. 6, adds to this the wilderness tradition, with the giving of the manna (cf. the reference to the Supper in John 6:53–58), and Heb. 8:8–13 includes reference to the new covenant of Jer. 31:31–34. The interpretation of Jesus' death therefore draws on a wide range of Old Testament traditions connected with the salvation history of Israel.

d. Jesus' Death and the Levitical Sacrificial System

As we delve further, it is clear that in some of the New Testament traditions there is also the interpretation of Christ's death in terms of the Old Testament Levitical sacrificial system of burnt offerings (Eph. 5:2), sin offerings (I John 1:7; 2:2; 4:10), and the Day of Atonement (Heb. 2:17; 9:6–15). Thus, in the latter passage from The Letter to the Hebrews, Christ is not only the perfect High Priest, which we shall discuss in a moment, but also the unblemished sacrificial victim offered once for all for the forgiveness of sins (so too in Heb. 10:12).

It is these three complexes of tradition from the Old Testament—the traditions of the exodus and Passover, of the Sinai covenant, and of the Levitical sacrificial and atonement system—which various New Testament writers use to interpret the significance of Christ's death on the cross. It is the Old Testament which is used, once again, to tell what Jesus has done.

e. Jesus and Melchizedek

This is equally true with respect to the isolated tradition in The Letter to the Hebrews, which terms Jesus a High Priest forever "after the order of Melchizedek" (Heb. 5:6, 10; 6:20; 7:11, 15, 17). The writer of Hebrews has taken over this title from the royal Psalm 110 (v. 4) and Gen. 14:17–20 (cf. Heb. 7:1–10) and has used it to connect Jesus' royal function as the Son of God with his sacrificial death (cf. Heb. 5:5–10; 7:26–28). In the Old Testament, Melchizedek was the ancient priest-king of Salem, the Jebusite fortress which David made his capital of Jerusalem, and from the time of David on, the ancient Jebusite-Canaanite traditions of Salem passed in to the traditions of Yahwism and affected the views of Yahweh, of Jerusalem, and of the king.[34] Hebrews therefore here reaffirms the application to Jesus of the royal Davidic titles, and at the same time selects a concept with which it can give witness to the superior and final sacrifice offered by Jesus, the perfect High Priest, who is "holy, blameless, unstained, separated from sinners, exalted above the heavens" (Heb. 7:26).

f. The Portrayal of the Crucifixion

A few other uses of Old Testament traditions in connection with Jesus' death must be mentioned. First, the events of the crucifixion reminded the Gospel writers of the suffering of the pious righteous as portrayed in some of the individual laments in the Psalter, and it was therefore in the colors of these laments that they pictured the crucifixion.

Psalm 22 served primarily for this purpose. The cry from

the cross (Mark 15:34 and par.; Ps. 22:1), the division of Jesus' garments and casting of lots for them (Mark 15:24 and par.; John 19:24; Ps. 22:18), the derision by the passersby, the mockery by the chief priests and scribes (Mark 15:29 and par., 31 and par.; Ps. 22:7–8), and Jesus' thirst (John 19:28; Ps. 22:15) —all were sketched out in the language of Ps. 22.

The individual lament of Ps. 69, with its reference to vinegar for drink (Ps. 69:21), was also used (Mark 15:23 and par., 36 and par.; John 19:29–30), as were Ps. 38:11 (Luke 23:49) and Ps. 31:5 (Luke 23:46). In addition, the writer of John found a fulfillment of the individual thanksgiving of Ps. 34:20 in the fact that Jesus' legs were not broken (John 19:36), and he made an allusion to Jesus' royal office in the description of the myrrh and aloes used to prepare Jesus' body for burial (John 19:39; cf. Ps. 45:8).

Similarly, the writer of John made some use of Zechariah (John 19:37; Zech. 12:10), as did Matthew (Matt. 27:9–10; Zech. 11:12–13; Jer. 32:6–15 and Jer. 18:2–3 were also employed), while Luke quoted Hosea (Luke 23:30; Hos. 10:8).

g. Jesus' Death in the Light of Ps. 118 and Isa. 8:13–15

Beyond these uses of Old Testament allusions and quotations within the passion story itself, however, a passage from one psalm of thanksgiving was used to interpret the whole event of the death and resurrection of Jesus. This was v. 22 of Ps. 118: Jesus was the "stone which the builders rejected" who had "become the head of the corner." This interpretation is found already in Mark's parable of the wicked tenants (Mark 12:1–12 and par.) and then appears again in Acts 4:11 and I Peter 2:7. Fuller has maintained that this use of Ps. 118:22 was the earliest interpretation of Jesus' death and resurrection used in the Palestinian church, but there seems scanty evidence for this.[35]

In addition, Paul interprets Jesus' death in terms of the stumbling stone of Isa. 8:13–15 (Rom. 9:32–33; I Cor. 1:23), and again I Peter, ch. 2, uses this interpretation (I Peter 2:8; cf. also Luke 2:34). But as we shall see in the next section, all these references to Jesus as a "cornerstone" or "stumbling stone" seem to imply a further understanding of Jesus in terms of the cornerstone of Isa. 28:16, and in fact are combined with that understanding in both Romans and I Peter.

It is clear, however, that Jesus' death was interpreted in many of the New Testament's traditions in the language and the light of the Old. To explain what had happened on the cross, many of the New Testament writers found the Old Testament indispensable.

5. *The Kerygma of the Incarnation*

As we have seen, there are a variety of ways by which the writers of the New Testament proclaimed who Jesus of Nazareth was and what he did, but none of these ways makes that proclamation more emphatic than does the incarnational theology of the New Testament, which is represented most fully in The Gospel According to John. Witnesses to Jesus which are only suggestive in the earlier traditions are expanded on and thought through to their full implications, especially in the Fourth Gospel, almost as if John desires to give us the mature product of the church's ongoing experience of the risen Christ. Let us illustrate.

There is in both Mark (Mark 14:58; 15:29) and Acts (Acts 6:14) the charge leveled against Jesus that he said he would destroy the Temple, and in the Marcan pericopes it is added that Jesus said he would rebuild the Temple in three days. It may be that such charges are thought to be false in these traditions.

In addition, in Rom. 9:33 and 10:11, part of Isa. 28:16 is quoted to refer to Jesus, and in Eph. 2:20, Jesus is the "cornerstone." That is, Romans and Ephesians suggest at least that Jesus is the cornerstone of the new congregation of faith, or the cornerstone of the new temple on Zion, as envisioned in the prophecy of Isaiah.

What do the later writers make of these two sets of tradition? First, in The Gospel According to John, the claim to destroy and rebuild the Temple in three days is placed in Jesus' mouth at the time of the Temple-cleansing (John 2:19), and John points out (John 2:21) that it is his own body to which Jesus refers. In John 4:21, then, Jesus tells the Samaritan woman that he will replace the temples on Zion and Gerizim and thus become the one way to the Father. In short, Jesus is understood as the new temple incarnate. Using the other approach, the writer of I Peter 2:4–8 understands Jesus as the incarnate cornerstone of the new congregation of faith, which was promised in Isa. 28:16, and that passage is quoted together with Ps. 118:22 and Isa. 8:14–15, thus bringing together all the references to Jesus as the "stone" or "cornerstone." But the intent is the same as that in John: Jesus is understood to have replaced the center of Jewish worship, by incarnating it in his person.

The same movement in the traditions toward their final interpretation in the incarnation can be discerned with regard to Jesus' Sonship. There is some suggestion in Matthew and Luke that Jesus was thought of as the embodiment of Israel, or at least as taking over Israel's role. In Matt. 2:15, this is expressed by referring the saying of Hos. 11:1 to Jesus: he becomes the Son of God who is called out of Egypt, replacing the nation Israel, which is often called the son of God in the Old Testament.[36] And in Luke's account of the transfiguration, Jesus speaks to Moses and Elijah about his "exodus" (Luke 9:31; "departure" in the RSV), which he is to accomplish in his crucifixion, again implying that Jesus has taken over the role of Israel. Similarly, there may be the intention in the Q account of the temptation in the wilderness (Matt. 4:3–11 and par.) deliberately to contrast the obedience of Jesus, the Son of God, with the disobedience of the first son, the people Israel, during its wilderness wanderings. In the Gospel of John, however, Jesus is "the only Son" (John 1:14, 18), entirely replacing the sonship of the Jews, who are children neither of Abraham (John 8:39 f.) nor of God (John 8:42) because of their constant disbelief. This replacement of Israel is then emphasized in another figure in John 15:1: Jesus is the "true vine," replacing the "vine" of Israel in the Old Testament (Ps. 80:8–15), which the prophets said became rotten (Isa. 5:1–7; cf. Hos. 10:1 ff.). In the view of the Fourth Gospel, Jesus in his incarnation becomes Israel, the only Son of God.

We have already referred to John's use of the Servant Songs of Second Isaiah in reference to Jesus as the light of the world and as the lamb of God—both portrayals in which the Servant's (Israel's) role becomes embodied in Jesus' person, indeed, both portrayals in which the Servant-Israel has been replaced by Jesus. It seems apparent that this replacement of Israel by the incarnation also lies behind John's understanding of the Supper.

In John's version of the Supper (John, ch. 13), no broken bread or cup is offered, but rather Jesus washes his disciples' feet, and the Passover does not take place until the crucifixion. In the earlier traditions of both Paul and Mark, the Supper had been the Passover meal, at which time the bread and the cup of the new covenant had been given (I Cor. 11:24–25; Mark 14:22–24 and par.). Further, although the exodus-Sinai traditions certainly lie behind the understanding of the cup in Paul and Mark, as we have said, there may also be reference to the fact that the Servant was to be the "covenant to the people" (Isa. 42:6), and the cup represents Jesus' blood which will be shed in his role as the Suffering Servant. In John, however, Jesus has totally replaced the Servant-Israel. He now is that figure incarnate, and thus, that which is offered is no longer bread or cup, but only Jesus himself. Now the way into the life of the new covenant is no longer via Jewish bread and wine, but solely via Jesus. He is "the living bread" (John 6:51) and he is "drink indeed" (John 6:55), and all that is needful is to abide in him. He has totally replaced the Servant-Israel in the working of God.

As the Son of God, as the true vine, as the Servant and light and lamb and covenant to the nations, as the one way to the Father, Jesus is the incarnate replacement of Israel according to the Fourth Gospel, the one who fulfills and completes Israel's role and therefore who makes Israel, and indeed Israel's

108

temple, subsequently unnecessary. It is as if these traditions of the Old Testament are here gathered up and given their final interpretation in terms of the incarnation.

The fact that such an interpretation is possible in the Fourth Gospel must mean that there were already strong incarnational tendencies in the Old Testament itself, and with respect to the Old Testament traditions which John uses, this is certainly the case. It all remains a future hope in the Old Testament, but certainly Isa. 28:16 looks forward to an incarnate cornerstone, a new congregation of faith on Zion, and certainly the Servant in Second Isaiah will be an incarnate covenant, an incarnate light to the nations, and an incarnate sacrifice for sin. John simply points to Jesus as the one in whom these future hopes have become reality.

Sometimes overlooked is the fact that already in the Old Testament there is a strong tendency toward the incarnation of the Word of God, in the portrayal of some of the prophets. In both Jeremiah and Ezekiel it is said that the prophet "eats" the word of God (Jer. 15:16; Ezek. 2:8 to 3:3), that is, the Word of God becomes part of the prophet's physical being, and the suffering which the prophet undergoes then is due to this identification of the prophet's being with the internalized word (cf. Jer. 15:17; 20:9; 4:19; cf. Isa. 21:2–4). This is especially true with regard to Ezekiel. Having taken the word within himself, he finds that it has become the ruler of his physical being. It binds him like cords (Ezek. 3:25), it makes him dumb (Ezek. 3:26–27), it brings the punishment of Israel physically upon him, so that he cannot turn from side to side (Ezek. 4:4–8), so that he "eats and drinks" the judgment upon Jerusalem (Ezek. 4:9–17), and suffers in his own life the loss of what Israel loses (Ezek. 12:1–20; 24:15–18). This is not the full incarnation of the word, in any sense of the term, since the word always remains distinct from Ezekiel, but it certainly is the movement toward the full embodiment of the word.

It is the final goal of this movement which The Gospel According to John announces has been reached in Jesus of

Nazareth. He is finally, in John, the incarnation of the word of God. Certainly this proclamation goes far beyond any Old Testament expectation. The Word/Son is understood as pre-existent,[37] and there is definite movement toward the later Trinitarian formula of the church in the presentation of the person of the Spirit. Nevertheless, it seems clear that the primary understanding of the incarnation of the word is in terms of the Old Testament, and that John, ch. 1, is a deliberate patterning after Gen., ch. 1. In both traditions, the word is the sole agent of creation, that which gives light and life, that which shines in the darkness and the darkness cannot overcome it.[38] John here understands the Word of God incarnate as the word of the Old Testament made flesh, and thus in John 1:45 he sums up this understanding in the words of Philip: "We have found him of whom Moses in the law and also the prophets wrote, Jesus of Nazareth, the son of Joseph." It is a different understanding from that of Heb. 1:1–2, where the speaking by the Son is something new from God's speaking in the past by the prophets. In John, that which was spoken by the prophets and by Moses is summed up and made flesh and spoken in the Christ. Jesus becomes the incarnation of the Old Testament promises, their fulfillment, and their end, as we have shown. It is in this light, therefore, that the cry of Jesus on the cross, according to John, is "It is finished" (John 19:30). The Old Testament salvation history has been brought to its conclusion.

There is another understanding of the person of Jesus to which we must point in a discussion of the incarnation—that of the witness to Jesus as the incarnation of the Promised Land, in The Letter to the Hebrews. In Heb. 3:7 to 4:13 there is a long admonitory section which exhorts the readers to hold fast their faith to the end and states that the reward of this faithfulness will be the entrance into the "rest" which God has promised to his people. In support of this admonition, Gen. 2:2 is quoted (Heb. 4:4) to show that God has set aside or hallowed a period of rest for his own, and reference is made to the fact that, in the Old Testament, the people of God failed to enter into the rest promised to them, because of their disobedience in the wilderness (cf. Ps. 95:8–11; Num. 14:1–35; Deut. 1:34–35).

This motif of "rest" is quite prominent in the Hexateuch, and everywhere is synonymous with Israel's entrance and settlement in the Promised Land. After the incident of the golden calf, Yahweh nevertheless promises Israel through Moses, "My presence will go with you, and I will give you rest" (Ex. 33:14). However, when Israel murmurs against Yahweh in the wilderness, Yahweh swears that none of Israel's first generation shall see the land promised to the fathers (Num. 14:22; Deut. 1:34–35; Ps. 95:11). But then, under the leadership of Joshua, the second generation of Israelites is led into the land, and the viewpoint of the D editor is that "now the LORD your God has given rest to your brethren, as he promised them" (Josh. 22:4; cf. chs. 21:44; 11:23). Further, in the thought of Deuteronomy, the fulfillment of the promise to the patriarchs of the land always includes the promise that Israel will have "rest from all . . . enemies round about" (Deut. 12:10; 25:19). The gift of the land is synonymous with the gift of "rest," and the land becomes the place where Israel finally enters into that period of "rest" first set aside and hallowed by Yahweh in his creation of the world (Gen. 2:2–3; Ex. 20:11; 31:17).

Certainly the writer of The Letter to the Hebrews could no longer speak of a *place* promised to the people of God, because the new Israel of the church transcended all bounds of geography. But he could and did still speak of the promised "rest" originally connected with the Promised Land, and he did so in incarnational terms. Now the "rest" was no longer connected with a place, but with a person. Now the rest was inherited through faith in Christ (Heb. 3:14). He became the way to the rest; indeed, in him the rest was to be found; in him, a "sabbath rest" was held out before the pilgrim people of God (Heb. 4:9; cf. Rev. 14:13), and the story of Israel's disobedience in the wilderness became the warning to the new Israel not to fail to enter this new rest which God offered. Thus, in

111

this isolated tradition of The Letter to the Hebrews, Jesus replaced the Promised Land. In comparison with the prominence of the land in the Old Testament, this New Testament use of the tradition seems minor. Nevertheless, it is there in the kerygma of the incarnation and is not to be overlooked.

6. *The Fulfillment of the Old Testament in the New*

Let us return to the question with which we first began this section: What happened to the ancient words and promises of the Old Testament? Did God keep his word? Did he bring it to fulfillment? In the light of the evidence that we have assembled above, we must say that the New Testament writers were sure that he did. Although their testimonies are of the greatest variety, the various New Testament authors pointed to Jesus of Nazareth as the one in whom the tradition histories of the Old Testament found their completion and fulfillment. For those who dealt with the royal traditions of the Old Testament, Jesus was variously the Messiah, the long-awaited son of David, the shepherd-prince promised by Ezekiel, the High Priest after the order of Melchizedek, who had been designated Son of God and exalted to the right hand of the Father as the Lord over all enemies and powers. He was the one to whom the traditions of David and the royal psalms pointed, the ruler whose coming inaugurated the beginning of the Kingdom of God.

For those who told the story of Jesus' earthly life and death, Jesus was diversely a new Moses, the prophet like Moses who was to come, the Suffering Servant who gave his life as a ransom for many. He was the one who freed Israel from her final slavery, who instituted the new Sinai covenant of the prophets in his blood, who made the perfect sacrifice for sin once for all. He was the stone which the builders rejected, which had become the head of the corner, the rock of stumbling for the Jews and foolishness for the Gentiles. He was the ideal righteous man of The Psalms, suffering and praising his Father from the cross. The traditions of exodus, Passover, and

Sinai, the Hexateuchal and the prophetic traditions, found their goal in him, and that plan which God began with his first release of his people from Egypt was brought to completion in the story of the crucifixion and resurrection.

For those who concentrated on the fullness of his incarnation, Jesus was, in various traditions, the new obedient son Israel, the incarnate temple or the cornerstone of the new congregation of faith on Zion, the incarnate covenant and light and lamb in his role as the Servant, the true vine, the true manna, the bread and drink of life. Indeed, he was the Word of the Old Testament made flesh, which gave the light that shone in the darkness. And he was the incarnate Promised Land, the place of rest offered to all who faithfully held fast to him.

Little of this witness to Jesus is unified in the New Testament. As we have seen, the different writers have their different emphases and their different proclamations of just who Jesus of Nazareth was and what it was he did. They call on different Old Testament traditions to give their testimonies to his person. And yet, all centers around that one figure of Jesus, and out of this multifaceted proclamation the fullness of the church's gospel is constructed. The modern preacher who would proclaim Jesus Christ is presented with all these various traditions, and all of them can serve as legitimate parts of the proclamation of the gospel. No one of them is complete in itself. But taken together, they present the good news of Jesus Christ to us in all its fullness.

The point we would emphasize, however, is that all these witnesses to Jesus of Nazareth have their roots in the Old Testament. All of them see that which God accomplished in Christ as the completion of a work God began in the history of Israel. And none of them can really be understood apart from that history. Jesus of Nazareth and his work have meaning, according to the New Testament, only in relation to Israel, and unless the modern preacher makes that relation clear, he cannot preach Jesus Christ as the New Testament writers knew and understood him.

113

Apart from his relation to Israel, Jesus could have been understood in the first- to third-century Mediterranean world as another mythical Savior in a mystery religion or Gnostic sect. But the fact that Jesus was understood in various ways as the fulfillment of Israel's history prevented his person and work from becoming the subjects simply of Gnostic doctrine or of endless superstition and speculation. Jesus was, the New Testament writers asserted in all their differing ways, tied to a concrete history of the past which had been completed in concrete events in the writers' age. And it was the sum total of those events, the writers said, which alone defined Jesus Christ.

As a result, time and again we hear in the various New Testament traditions that Jesus fulfills the Old:

The Son of man goes as it is written of him. (Mark 14:21 and par.; cf. chs. 8:31 and par.; 9:12.)

Christ died for our sins in accordance with the scriptures, . . . he was raised on the third day in accordance with the scriptures. (I Cor. 15:3; cf. Rom. 1:2; 3:21.)

These are my words which I spoke to you, while I was still with you, that everything written about me in the law of Moses and the prophets and the psalms must be fulfilled. Then he opened their minds to understand the scriptures. (Luke 24:44–45; cf. chs. 24:27; 1:32–33, 46–55, 68–79; 2:29–32.)

But all this has taken place, that the scriptures of the prophets might be fulfilled. (Matt. 26:56.)

And when they had fulfilled all that was written of him, they took him down from the tree, and laid him in a tomb. (Acts 13:29; cf. chs. 3:18; 18:28; 26:22–23; 28:23.)

We have found him of whom Moses in the law and also the prophets wrote. (John 1:45.)

The prophets who prophesied of the grace that was to be yours searched and inquired about this salvation; they inquired what person or time was indicated by the Spirit of

Christ within them when predicting the sufferings of Christ and the subsequent glory. (I Peter 1:10–11.)

Indeed, in The Gospel According to Matthew, the writer repeatedly understands the events of Jesus' life as the fulfillment of the Old Testament history.[39]

This is not to say that there is not also in various New Testament traditions a sense of the newness of God's act in Jesus Christ and therefore an inability to comprehend Jesus of Nazareth simply in terms of the Old Testament. With the appearance of Jesus, something greater than Solomon and Jonah (Luke 11:31–32) and even Abraham (John 8:53–59) and Moses (Mark 9:2–8 and par.; Matt. 5:21–48; John 1:17) is present. Jesus brings with him the beginning of that new age for which the old Israel could only hope (Matt. 13:16–17 and par.), and the participants in that new age become greater than even the greatest of the prophets (Matt. 11:11 and par.).

Yet, as was the case with the working of the word in the Old Testament, the inbreaking of a new action of God in the new word in Jesus Christ does not abrogate the old. Rather, the new gathers up the old and brings it to completion and thereby gives the old a new interpretation. The final meaning of the promises and words of the Old Testament finds their final goal and interpretation in the life and death and resurrection of Jesus Christ. But it is precisely those old words which are used to tell who this new Word is, and without the old the new cannot be truly proclaimed.

If, then, the preacher of the present day wishes to proclaim the good news of Jesus Christ, he is also going to have to proclaim the words and promises of the Old Testament. Only if this is done will our congregations know who Jesus Christ is. Jesus Christ is not some mysterious figure, suddenly appearing from the blue. He is not an ideal divorced from history, or simply a projection of theological speculation. He is not a myth or a symbol of a new self-understanding on the part of man. He is not a humanistic model of a righteous man for others. Jesus Christ is the fulfillment of God's word to Israel. He is the

115

completion and reinterpretation of Israel's two thousand years of history with her God. He is God's act whereby he brings his salvation histories to their end and begins a new one. If we would be true to the New Testament, then we must proclaim Jesus Christ as the New Testament writers proclaimed him—in terms of God's history with Israel and the fulfillment of that history. Only so can the modern preacher make clear to his people just who Jesus Christ is and what it is he has done.

C. THE HISTORICAL ANALOGY
OF ISRAEL AND THE CHURCH

It is also only in the light of the Old Testament that the present-day preacher can make clear the New Testament understanding of the church.

There are several different understandings of the nature of the church in the New Testament. In Paul's writings, the church is the body of Christ (I Cor. 12:12, 27; Rom. 12:5; cf. Eph. 1:23; 4:12; 5:30; Col. 1:18, 24) and the temple for the Spirit of God (I Cor. 3:16–17; cf. Eph. 2:22). But the church is also "the household of faith" (Gal. 6:10; cf. Eph. 2:19; I Tim. 3:15), and this is similar to the thought in Heb. 3:6 that the church is "God's house," or to the view in I Peter 2:5 that it is the "spiritual house" into which believers are built as "living stones," Christ being that cornerstone of Isa. 28:16, which we discussed before (cf. I Cor. 3:9–11).

It is therefore not surprising that these New Testament writers consider the church to be the heir of the promises to Israel. Because in Jesus Christ the Old Testament story is brought to its completion—as Paul puts it, "All the promises of God find their Yes in him" (II Cor. 1:20)—therefore the followers of Jesus Christ are those who inherit the fulfillment of the promises to Israel; indeed, it is they who become the new Israel in Christ. Let us see how this is expressed in the various New Testament traditions.

It is in the letters of Paul, the missionary to the Gentiles, surprisingly enough, that the church's role as the new Israel is most fully expressed. Once, in Gal. 6:16, the followers of Christ are called "the Israel of God," and it is clear in that letter that Paul considers the true sons of Abraham to be those who believe in Christ (Gal. 3:7; cf. Rom., chs. 4; 9:6–8). As such, they become the inheritors of the promise to Abraham, "In you shall all the nations be blessed" (Gen. 12:3; Gal. 3:8; cf. Rom. 15:8; Acts 3:25), receiving the promised blessing; they become the new people of God envisioned by Hosea (Rom. 9:25–26; Hos. 2:23; 1:10; cf. I Peter 2:10); they become the saved remnant foreseen by Isaiah (Rom. 9:27; Isa. 10:22–23). For as it is put in Gal. 3:29, "If you are Christ's, then you are Abraham's offspring, heirs according to promise," and the promises made to Israel then become the possession of the church. As it is similarly stated in the separate tradition of Heb. 4:9, it is the church which has become "the people of God."

For this reason, Paul can call the followers of Christ "the true circumcision" (Phil. 3:3; cf. Rom. 2:28–29; Col. 2:11), i.e., it is those of faith who truly belong to Israel. In the same manner, those of Christ are "God's elect" (Rom. 8:33), those whom God has called (Rom. 1:7; 9:24; cf. Mark 13:22, 27 and par.). They are the *ecclesia,* the gathered people of God (I Cor. 10:32; 15:9; II Cor. 1:1; Gal. 1:13; Phil. 3:6; cf. Acts 5:11; 8:1, 3). Unlike the old Israel, the former people of God with its center in Jerusalem, the new Israel in Christ has a Jerusalem that is above (Gal. 4:26), a commonwealth in heaven (Phil. 3:20; cf. Heb. 12:22; Rev., ch. 21). The church has, according to all these passages, inherited the role of Israel, and in Christ it has become the recipient of the promises given to Israel in the Old Testament.

On this basis, Paul could therefore speak of Gentile Christians as the wild branches which had been grafted into the tree and root of Israel (Rom. 11:17–20). And Eph. 2:12 could compare the Gentiles' former separation from Christ to an alienation also from the commonwealth of Israel.

This means, further, that it was through Christ that the church inherited the Old Testament as its Scripture. The words and promises of the Old Testament had been addressed to Israel and to Israel alone, as Paul acknowledges in Rom. 9:4–5. But because in Christ the church had become the people of God, the new Israel, it could understand the Word of God as addressed henceforth to it:

> For whatever was written in former days was written for our instruction. (Rom. 15:4; cf. ch. 4:23–24.)

The Old Testament had meaning because it was fulfilled in Christ (cf. II Tim. 3:14–16); its prophetic word had been "made more sure" (II Peter 1:19); its history had culminated in the life and death and resurrection of Jesus of Nazareth. As the new Israel in Christ, the church had a historical connection with the old Israel. God's salvation histories had issued in the fulfillment of his promises, in the creation of that new people, through Christ, which the prophets had envisioned. The word addressed to Israel therefore became the word addressed to the church, and the Old Testament became an inseparable part of the church's canon.

As the new Israel in Christ, the church not only inherited the fulfillment of the Old Testament but the church's life was an amazing analogy to the life of the old Israel. The prophets of the Old Testament had envisioned that the life of the new people of God would to some extent reenact the history of the former Israel (see Ch. IV), and according to some of the writers of the New Testament, this was exactly the case. Let us examine some of these parallels between the old Israel's life and the new, as they present themselves in the various traditions.

First of all, it is quite clear in Paul's letters that he considers Christ's death on the cross as the parallel to the Old Testament event of the exodus, as we have seen. Christ's death, the sacrifice of the Paschal lamb (I Cor. 5:7), was the redemption price paid to free the Christian from slavery to sin and the law and to give him adoption as a son of God (I Cor. 6:20; 7:23; Gal. 4:4–7), exactly as Israel was redeemed in the

118

exodus from Egypt and made the son of God. It is Paul's conception, then, that the Christian participates in the death of Christ and receives the redemption from slavery, i.e., undergoes the exodus, through the gift of baptism (Rom. 6:3–14; 7:4–6; Gal. 3:26–27; cf. I Cor. 10:2; Col. 2:12–15).[40] With his baptism into Christ's death, the Christian participates in his own exodus event.

Further, it is clear in both I Cor. 11:23–26 and Mark 14:22–24 and par. that participation in the Lord's Supper constituted for the Christian the parallel to Israel's entrance into the covenant with Yahweh. The cup is the covenant in Christ's blood, and forms not only the historical analogy to the covenant on Sinai but also the fulfillment of the prophetic promise of a new covenant of God with his people (cf. Heb. 8:8–12; 10:15–17, which quote Jer. 31:31–34). So it is that I Peter 2:9 can quote the words of Ex. 19:6, spoken to Israel at Sinai, in relation to the church which has become a kingdom of priests (cf. Rev. 1:6), a holy nation, God's own people.

On the basis of these analogies, we can say that the church and Israel both were redeemed out of slavery and made sons of God, with no deserving on their part, but solely out of the mercy and love of God (Deut. 7:6–8; Rom. 5:6). Both were brought to the table of the Lord to eat and drink with him and to enter into covenant with him as his chosen people (Ex. 24:1–11). Both were thereby given "the glorious liberty of the children of God" (Rom. 8:21), delivered into a new life of freedom, and set on their way toward the fulfillment of God's promises. Both were pilgrim people, in the thought of The Letter to the Hebrews, seeking that "city which has foundations, whose builder and maker is God" (Heb. 11:10, 16; 13:14; cf. ch. 10:34); or in the traditions of the Promised Land, both journeyed toward that "homeland" (Heb. 11:14) and "rest" (Heb. 3:7 to 4:13) which was originally promised to the fathers.

Because the church's life was analogous to the life of Israel in the Old Testament, the experiences which Israel had could

119

also serve as warnings to the church, and both Hebrews (Heb. 3:7–19) and Paul use the history of Israel in this manner (I Cor. 10:1–13). As Paul puts it:

Now these things happened to them as a warning, but they were written down for our instruction, upon whom the end of the ages has come. (I Cor. 10:11.)

Other analogies can be drawn between Israel and the church on the basis of various traditions in the two Testaments. Just as Israel had been set apart for the special purpose of God [41] (Num. 23:9; Ex. 33:16), so the church was also set apart from the world (Rom. 12:2; Gal. 1:4; cf. I Peter 1:14–16; Matt. 13:22; I John 2:15; Eph. 4:22). Like Israel, the church was not to follow the customs and laws of the world (Lev. 18:1–5; cf. Ezek. 20:32; I Sam. 8:4–9, 19–20): worldly distinctions (Gal. 3:27–28; II Cor. 5:17; Col. 3:11), wisdom (I Cor. 1:18 to 4:20), laws (Matt., chs. 5 to 7; I Cor., chs. 8 to 10) were done away, and all was to be done only to the glory of God (I Cor. 10:31).

The church was not to reject the world entirely, any more than Israel rejected it. The people of God as a whole never saw their life in terms of a mystical or ascetic escape from history.[42] But the church, like Israel, was to reject the ways of the world, "the works of darkness" (I Thess. 5:1–11; Rom. 13:11–14; Eph. 5:1–20; I John 2:7–11), and to walk only in the commandments of God, as "sons of light" (I Thess. 5:5; cf. Isa. 2:5).

A new day had dawned, a new age had begun (II Cor. 5:16–17; Col. 1:13; Heb. 6:5; I Peter 1:3–4, 23; John 3:3). God had entered history in a decisive new act, as he had entered it in the time of Moses and David, and as he had promised to enter it in the words of the prophets. He had chosen for himself a people, and delivered them from bondage, and given them a new life of freedom and a new set of circumstances, and set them on a new way toward the fulfillment of his word. And as God accompanied Israel on her journey toward the Promised Land (Ex. 33:12–16), so he accompanied the church on its pilgrimage. His presence with his church, according to Acts, was made known by the gift of the Spirit (Acts 2:14–21, 38;

5:32; 8:14–17; 10:44–48). Indeed, for Paul, the mark of the church was that God was with it in his Spirit (Rom. 8:9–11; I Cor. 3:16; II Cor. 13:14; Gal. 3:2; Phil. 2:1; cf. Eph. 2:22).[43] But the gift of the Spirit was but the firstfruit of the age to come (Rom. 8:23), the guarantee that God would fulfill his promise to the church (II Cor. 1:22; 5:5), the foretaste of God's final Kingdom to come. In that Spirit, the church journeyed toward God's promised goal of the Kingdom (cf. II Cor. 4:13 to 5:5), as Israel journeyed toward its Promised Land.

To cite further parallels, the church was understood in several of the traditions as the bride of Christ (e.g., II Cor. 11:2; Eph. 5:31–32), just as Israel had been the bride of God in her journey through the wilderness (Hos. 2:14–20; Jer. 2:2).

In other passages, it was stated that, like Israel, the church offered sacrifices to God, but now these were the "spiritual sacrifices" (I Peter 2:5) of praise (Heb. 13:15) and service (Rom. 12:1), which replaced the Israelite cult that had once and for all, according to Hebrews, been fulfilled in Christ.

Acts recorded that the church, like Israel, experienced the rise of prophets (Acts 11:27–30; 21:7–14), who were able to speak the word of God in the Spirit (Acts 4:31; 6:5) and to perform works of power (Acts 6:8).

Also in Luke's writings, the church considered itself, like Israel, to have a special link to Jerusalem, although this is contradicted in Mark's Gospel. In Mark, Jerusalem is a place of hostility, and the risen Christ manifests himself only in Galilee among the Gentiles (Mark 16:7). But according to Luke, Jesus appears to his disciples after his resurrection, in Jerusalem (Luke 24:36–49), he commands them to remain there until they receive the gift of the Spirit (Luke 24:49, cf. vs. 52–53), and from there the church is extended into the Gentile world (cf. Acts).

Finally, many of the traditions understood the church, like Israel, to have a mission to the world, although there are basic differences in the Old and New Testament understandings at this point. In the Old Testament, the creation of Israel was for the purpose of bringing blessing on all nations (Gen. 12:3),

121

and this purpose was ultimately to be fulfilled by the inclusion of the nations in Israel, according to the prophets. But only in The Book of Jonah do we find any active missionary role on the part of Israel or her prophets.[44] The primary understanding, exhibited in Second Isaiah, is that the nations will come to Israel because of the salvation manifested in her. There is no thought that Israel herself will take the good news to the world. The revelation to the nations remains an act accomplished solely by God in his redemption of his people.

In many of the New Testament traditions, however, the new Israel in Christ is engaged in active missionary endeavor. Jesus' disciples are sent not only to the Jews (Mark 6:7–13 and par.; Acts 3:25) and the Samaritans (Luke 10:1–20 and par.; Matt. 10:7–16) to gather together God's chosen people. The promise is also to those who are far off (Acts 2:39; Eph. 2:13, 17; Gal. 3:8); i.e., the Gentiles, who are not of Israel's fold (cf. John 10:16), and the followers of Christ are sent into the world (John 17:18, 20; 20:21) "to gather into one the children of God who are scattered abroad" (John 11:52). In Matt. 28:19, the specific command is to "go therefore and make disciples of all nations," or in Luke 24:47, to preach "repentance and forgiveness of sins . . . in his name to all nations, beginning from Jerusalem" (cf. Rom. 1:5). Nevertheless, there is striking correspondence between the life and function of Israel in the Old Testament and of the church in the New.

We must emphasize, however, that this correspondence, this analogy between the Old Israel and the new, has as its sole basis the salvation history, in which the church is understood as the realization of that new people of God, created in Christ, which was promised in the Old Testament. There is no other real historical relation between Israel and the church. They cannot be compared on the grounds that men are the same in every age and that therefore Israel's experience is instructive for the church—historians have shown us how relative to its time is the human personality. Israel and the church cannot be related by pointing out similar situations within their respective histories—the situation of the first- and second-century church in the New Testament is almost as different from that of ancient Israel as our modern situation is from that of the New Testament. Rather, ancient Israel and the New Testament church—and indeed the modern Christian church—are all related by one fact, by our common participation in the people of God. On that historical basis alone we share the same history: the history of redemption, in which we have been delivered from slavery by God, brought into covenant with him, given a new life, and then set on our way toward the fulfillment of his promises and purposes for us.

It is in that salvation history, which we share with Israel through our faith in Jesus Christ, that the Old Testament is given to us as the word of God directed also to us, as well as to ancient Israel, and as a guide and warning and indeed, as an analogous account of our journey toward the promised Kingdom.

It seems obvious, therefore, that if the modern preacher wants to instruct his people as to who they are and what their life as the people of God is all about and toward what goal they are heading, in a fashion commensurate with the New Testament proclamation, then he is going to have to proclaim the Old Testament word along with the New. We modern Christians have become members of the New Israel in Christ. We need, therefore, to know who Israel is. And our life in Christ is analogous in many respects to the life of Israel. It would be helpful therefore to know what Israel's pilgrimage was like as we journey onward in our own. Indeed, for the modern preacher to neglect such proclamation is to leave his people without a full understanding of their identity and to refuse to guide them along their way with the signposts and instructions that God has mercifully given us through two thousand years of relationship with our Israelite forebears. Our faith in Jesus Christ has brought us into the covenant people. Not to make known the nature of that unique, historical community is finally to ignore the full implications of the good news of Jesus Christ.

Part Three

PREACHING
FROM THE OLD TESTAMENT

Chapter VI

Removing the Obstacles
to the Word of the Lord

I T IS CLEAR from our previous discussion that the preacher who desires to proclaim Jesus Christ in terms consonant with the witness of the New Testament is going to have to include in his preaching the witness of the Old Testament as well, for Jesus Christ and his church cannot be understood apart from the Israel of God.

It is one thing to make that statement, however, and another to apply it. Few clergymen really are versed in a valid method of preaching from the Old Testament, and this deficiency has also contributed to the loss of the Old Testament in the church. We do not hear the Old Testament from our pulpits because our preachers do not know how to use it. In the words of Yahweh through Hosea:

> with you is my contention, O priest. . . .
> My people are destroyed for lack of knowledge;
> because you have rejected knowledge.
> (Hos. 4:4, 6.)

We therefore come down to the nitty-gritty of applying all that we have said to the actual preparation of sermons. Our previous discussion has many implications for homiletical methodology, and a valid methodology can be constructed only on the basis of such a discussion of the actual relationships between the two Testaments as we have tried to present. It is those relationships alone which dictate the way the Old Testament can be used. And it is those relationships which we will try to spell out in the practical terms of sermon construction.

A. CHOOSING A TEXT

Obviously the first step in sermon preparation is the selection of a text, and here we are faced with the question of what passages we should use from the Old Testament.

On the basis of our previous discussion, the whole Old Testament lies open to the Christian preacher as witness to the Word of God, for it is not merely the promises of the prophets which are fulfilled in Jesus Christ. All the tradition histories of the Old Testament are gathered up and brought to completion in him. Consequently, the whole of Israel's life as the people of God forms a historical analogy to the life of the church, and on this basis any portion of the Old Testament can be read as the story also of the Christian. If the preacher has the full knowledge of the Old Testament which he should have, he therefore confronts the treasures contained in the Old Testament of almost two thousand years of faith and witness, and he draws from an inexhaustible well of experience before God.

1. *The Use of a Lectionary*

Practically, most preachers will have to rely on someone else's lectionary, and usually they will turn to the lessons prescribed for their own denomination.

There is merit in this. The lectionaries set forth the course of the church year, and the regular round of Advent, Christmas, Epiphany, Lent, Easter, and Pentecost has always served as one of the most valuable teaching aids of the church. Furthermore, by following a prescribed lectionary, the preacher is steered away from his own subjectivism and forced to deal

128

with texts with which he otherwise might not deal. Every lectionary makes some effort, whether successful or not, to present the whole gospel.

Unfortunately, however, each denomination's lectionary is only as sound as the views of the committee who compiled it. The major denominations all periodically revise their lessons, and therefore there is not a good deal of agreement among them, especially in the recommendation of Old Testament lessons.[1] Each committee includes men who know more about one book of the Bible than some other, and these individual strengths show up in the choice of lessons,[2] as do the theological emphases of the committees' particular eras. In addition, the lectionary committees of some of the major denominations seem to have lacked any representative with a thoroughgoing knowledge of form criticism, and this has led to the recommendation of Old Testament lessons that either truncate or overextend the boundaries of the chosen Old Testament passages.[3] Worst of all, the choice of some passages seems inexplicable. Why should the account of Jeremiah's call, Jer. 1:4–10, 17–19, be read on the third Sunday in Advent,[4] for example, or Lev. 6:1–13 on the second Sunday after Easter?[5]

Clearly there is nothing binding about the recommended lectionaries, and they should be used selectively as guides but not as authorities. The preacher may consider their suggestions, but he should also bring the results of his own continual study of the Old Testament to bear on the evaluation of the lectionaries' recommendations. Further, every preacher would profit from an attempt to construct his own lectionary, for such an attempt gives one an insight into the necessities of the church year and vividly highlights what one is most tempted to leave out from one's preaching.

There is no possibility of covering, in fifty-two Sundays of the year, every portion of the Old Testament or even of the New. Lectionaries should therefore change from year to year and run in at least three-year cycles. Even then every facet of the gospel will not be proclaimed, and one must finally conclude that lectionaries should deal with the basics of the gospel, with the foundations of our faith. As is well stated in the Introduction to *Services of the Church,* issued in 1969 by the Commission on Worship of the United Church of Christ:

> By the use of selected Bible passages for reading in worship, and for interpretation through preaching, the people of God relive what he has done in the past and participate in what he is doing now. In this way the celebration of God's presence derives its chief meaning from the central event of human history—the life, death, and resurrection of Jesus Christ.[6]

2. *The Church Year*

The progress of the church year clearly divides itself into two parts: Advent through Ascension, when the story of the life, death, and resurrection of Jesus Christ is told, and Pentecost through the rest of the Sundays, when the implications and results of the gospel for the life of the people of God are spelled out. This is not a clear-cut division, of course, and in both parts it is the action of God which should form the basis of the proclamation. But both parts should be equally informed by the use of the Old Testament, to result in, to illumine, or to contrast with the New.

a. Advent

The Advent season deals with the coming of God to his people. Thus, those Old Testament texts which deal with the coming of God in both judgment and salvation are appropriate, and since it is the prophets who announced God's future eschatological appearance, it is from the prophetic writings that most Advent texts are drawn:[7]

> Amos 4:6–12—"Prepare to meet your God, O Israel!"
> Isa. 2:6–21—"The LORD alone will be exalted in that day."
> Isa. 33:7–16—"Who among us can dwell with the devouring fire?"
> Ezek. 12:21–28—"The days are at hand, and the fulfilment of every vision."

130

Ezek., ch. 34—"Behold, I, I myself will search for my sheep, and will seek them out."

Ezek. 37:24–28—"My dwelling place shall be with them."

Isa. 40:1–8—"The glory of the LORD shall be revealed."

Isa. 40:9–11—"Behold, the Lord GOD comes with might."

Mal. 3:1–12—"The Lord whom you seek will suddenly come to his temple."

Mal. 4:5–6—"Behold, I will send you Elijah the prophet before the great and terrible day of the LORD comes."

But Advent also deals with our situation of exile, under wrath, isolated from God, without hope:

Gen., ch. 3—"You are dust, and to dust you shall return."

Ps. 137—"How shall we sing the LORD's song in a foreign land?" [8]

Isa., ch. 64—"In our sins we have been a long time, and shall we be saved?"

Lam., ch. 5—"We have become orphans, fatherless."

b. Christmas

In the event of Christmas, then, it is announced that the Son of God is born, that all those promises of God remembered in the Old Testament have come to pass, and it is therefore this fulfillment which the Christmas use of the Old Testament must surely emphasize, the fact that Christmas is a celebration of the faithfulness of God:

Gen. 12:1–3—"In you all the families of the earth shall be blessed."

Num. 24:15–19—"A star shall come forth out of Jacob."

I Sam. 2:1–10—"I rejoice in thy salvation."

II Sam., ch. 7—"Your house and your kingdom shall be made sure for ever before me; your throne shall be established for ever."

Isa., ch. 7—"Behold, a young woman shall conceive and bear a son, and shall call his name Immanuel."

Isa. 8:16 to 9:7—"The people who walked in darkness have seen a great light."

Isa. 11:1–9—"There shall come forth a shoot from the stump of Jesse."

Jer. 23:5–6—"He shall reign as king and deal wisely, and shall execute justice and righteousness in the land."

Micah 5:2–4—"From you shall come forth for me one who is to be ruler in Israel."

Isa. 42:1–9—"Behold, the former things have come to pass, and new things I now declare."

Isa., ch. 55—"So shall my word be that goes forth from my mouth; it shall not return to me empty."

c. Epiphany

There are two Sundays after Christmas, followed by the Epiphany season of ten weeks before Ash Wednesday. Epiphany marks the revelation of our Lord to the nations, with the traditional reading of the story of the Wise Men from Matt. 2:1–12 and, very often, of the promise to Israel from Isa. 60: 1–7. Certainly Isa. 52:7–10 (12) would be just as appropriate. *The Book of Common Worship* imaginatively suggests I Kings 10:1–13 for this day, the story of the visit of the Queen of Sheba to Solomon, and this could serve as a fitting contrast to the Matthew story. For the first Sunday after Epiphany, *The Book of Common Prayer* designates Prov. 8:22–35, and again this is an imaginative use of the Old Testament: Jesus Christ is understood as the incarnation of that Wisdom which speaks in the Old Testament, a usage fully consonant with the New Testament.[9] On this basis, passages from Prov. 2:1–15 or 3:5–18 would also be appropriate. Perhaps Jer. 9:23–24 would be best of all, however.

We would suggest that during the long Epiphany season the preacher has one primary task—to proclaim who Jesus Christ is. Many people in the average congregation, if not most of them, actually do not know who it was who was born in Bethlehem, and, like the disciples of the early church, the preacher has the responsibility of making this clear.

It is at this time, then, that the long story of Israel can be told so meaningfully: the creation by God of a world which he intended to be very good; the disruption and ruin of that world by man's attempts to make God unnecessary; the calling of Abraham to be the beginning of a new people which would live justly and righteously under God's Lordship and draw all men into its fellowship; God's gift to that people of covenant and land and kingship and prophets; the unfaithfulness of that people despite God's constant mercy and faithfulness toward them; the rejection of Israel and the judgment upon her, but once again the promise of a new people, which finally found its embodiment and fulfillment in the person of Jesus Christ.

It is here that many of the texts from the Old Testament which we discussed in the previous section and some of which are used by the New Testament can be employed with fruitful results:

Jesus as the messianic Son of God and son of David—Ps. 2; II Sam., ch. 7.

Jesus as Israel, the obedient Son of God—Hos. 11:1–9; Deut. 8:1–10, especially in connection with Jesus' temptation.

Jesus as the new Moses—Ex. 2:1–10; 32:30–34; Deut. 4:9–24; 5:22–33; 9:6–29.

Jesus as the Mosaic prophet-servant—Deut. 18:15–22.

Jesus as the Servant of Second Isaiah—Isa. 42:1–4; 49:1–6; 50:4–9.

Jesus as the agent in creation—Gen. 1:1 to 2:4a.

Jesus as the incarnate Word—Gen. 1:1 to 2:4a; Deut. 6:4–9; Hos. 8:11–12 (by way of contrast); Isa. 51:1–3, 4–6, 7–8; Ezek. 12:21–25, 26–28; and many other passages from the prophets.

Jesus as the incarnate congregation of faith—Isa. 28:1–22.

Jesus as the incarnate land or place of rest—Gen. 2:1–3; Josh. 11:21–23; 21:43–45; chs. 23; 24:1–28.

Jesus as the promised shepherd—Ezek., chs. 34; 37:24–28.

Jesus as redeemer—Lev. 25:25–28, 47–55.

In dealing with Jesus Christ as the fulfillment of the Old Testament, both in the Epiphany season and in other seasons, the preacher can also call on motifs that run throughout both Testaments and that sometimes contrast the New Testament fulfillment with its Old Testament promise. For example, both Testaments have a garden (Gen., ch. 3; Mark 14:32–42 and par.), a vine (Ps. 80; Isa. 5:1–7; Jer. 6:9–15; Ezek., ch. 15; Hos. 10:1–8; 14:1–8; John 15:1–17; Mark 12:1–12 and par.), and food in the wilderness (Ex., ch. 16; Num. 11:4–34; Mark 6:30–44 and par.; John, ch. 6). Two of the most richly used figures are those of the yoke (Hos. 10:11–12; 11:1–4; cf. ch. 4:16; Jer. 2:20–22; 5:1–9; Lam. 1:14–16; 3:25–33; Matt. 11:28–30; cf. Gal. 5:1)[10] and of the cup (Isa. 51:17 to 52:12; Jer. 25:15–29; Ezek. 23:32–34; Hab. 2:15–17; Zech. 12:1–5; Mark 10:35–45 and par.; 14:22–25 and par.; Matt. 26:36–46; John 18:1–11; I Cor. 10:14–22; 11:23–32), and both can be employed with great meaning in relationship to discipleship and the covenant or the Lord's Supper. Similarly, there are the great motifs, spanning both Testaments, of the light (e.g., Ex. 10:21–23; Job, ch. 29) or of the living water (e.g., Isa. 8:5–8; Jer. 2:4–13; Ezek. 47:1–12; Ps. 46), or of the way (Isa. 30:19–26, especially, although there are hundreds of references), as there are the converse motifs of the chaos (e.g., Ps. 46; Jer. 4:23–26) and darkness (e.g., Jer. 13:15–17; Amos 5:18–20) and death (e.g., Jer. 9:20–22; Amos 5:1–17).

If the preacher uses one of these motifs to tell the story of salvation and thus to make clear who Jesus Christ is, it must be emphasized, however, that he is dealing with events that happened and not just with ideas. The point is, What happened in the first garden[11] and in the second? What did the cup of the wrath of the Lord become in the hands of Jesus Christ? What was the yoke that Israel broke and with what did God replace it, in the actual day-by-day living of the follower of Jesus? The figures of the Bible refer to God's actions in the salvation history, and they must never be reduced to the status of mere ideas and metaphors.

This means, in the second place, that the way the preacher

spells out the relationship of the Old Testament and the New Testament must also be very carefully controlled by the salvation history itself, as it is witnessed to in the passages under consideration. The preacher who would proclaim the Biblical message is not permitted wild flights of fancy and allegorical devices designed to relate the Testaments to each other or to our present life. Rather, the preacher is bounded by the sacred history of what really happened and what God actually did in relation to his people, and it is this which is set forth by the motifs common to both Testaments. We shall subsequently go into this at greater length. For the moment, let us return to the church year.

The season of Epiphany reaches its climax in the story of the transfiguration of our Lord, that is, in the revelation of his glory and coming exaltation, and once again Old Testament passages dealing with the glory of God can be used very effectively: Moses' wistful plea to see God's glory (Ex. 33:17–23); the reflection of the glory of God from the face of Moses (Ex. 34:29–35), to which Paul then refers in II Cor. 3:7 to 4:6; the descent of the glory of God to the tabernacle (Ex. 40:34–38), which is, for the Priestly writer, the fulfillment of the promise to Abraham; the promise of the revelation of the glory of God to all flesh (Isa. 40:1–5); the song of the seraphim (Isa. 6:1–12); or the great psalm dealing with the glory and might of Yahweh as related to his acts in nature (Ps. 29).

d. Lent

Following the Epiphany season are the three Sundays before Lent (in some calendars) and the Lenten season itself. Only if the people have come to some understanding of who Jesus Christ is will the Lenten days make any sense to them, for only if we have known the Lord do we become conscious of the demands he has laid upon us, of our sinful failure to meet those demands, and of the necessity of repentance and of his suffering and ours.

Temptation is a part of our concern during Lent, and where else are the many faces of temptation so illumined as in the

Old Testament: Gen., chs. 3; 4:1–16; 11:1–9; Ex. 5:1 to 6:1; Num. 14:1–10; Deut. 8:11–20; II Sam., ch. 11; I Kings 21:1–24; Isa. 3:16 to 4:1; Jer. 15:15–21; Hab. 1:12–17; Ps. 37; 73; etc.

In similar fashion, the Old Testament fully spells out the demands God lays upon us: Ex. 20:1–17; Lev. 19:1–18; Deut. 30:11–14, 15–20; Ps. 1; 15; Isa. 1:18–20; Hos. 5:15 to 6:6; Amos 6:1–7; Micah 6:6–8; and hundreds of passages.

The Old Testament uncovers our sin so well, especially in the preaching of the prophets: Isa. 1:2–6; 30:1–5, 8–17; 59:1–19; Jer. 5:1–9; 8:18 to 9:9; 6:9–15; Ezek. 22:1–16; Hos. 5:3–7; Micah 6:1–5; 7:1–7; Zeph. 3:1–13; Mal. 1:6–14; etc.; but also in the historical books and the Writings: Gen. 6:5–8; 12:10–20; 18:9–15; Ex., ch. 32; Num., chs. 11; 14:39–45; 21:4–9; Deut. 1:26–33; I Sam., ch. 8; II Sam. 12:1–15a; Job 42:1–6; Ps. 143; Eccl. 1:1–11; etc.

The Old Testament speaks unequivocally of the judgment of God upon our sin: Isa. 6:1–12; Ezek. 2:1–7; Jer. 12:7–13; Hos. 1:2–9; 2:2–13; Amos 9:1–4; and of the fast of repentance that is required of us: Isa., ch. 58; Hos. 14:1–8; Joel 2:1–14; Amos 5:14–15. It is clear, therefore, that the destruction of our sin in the judgment and the disciplining by God are necessary: Isa. 1:24–26; 4:2–6; 27:7–11; Jer. 15:5–9; Ezek. 20:1–38; 22:17–22; 24:6–14; Hos., ch. 3; Micah 5:10–15. And against this background, the necessity of the suffering of the Son of Man becomes clear.

But there is also that divine yearning of God for his people and the hope beyond the judgment: Isa. 49:14–21; 50:1–3; 54:4–8; Jer. 31:15–20, 23–25, 27–28, 31–34, 35–36, 37; ch. 32; Ezek. 36:22–32; 37:15–23; 39:25–29; Hos. 11:1–9. In this light, the mercy of the cross also can be understood.

e. Passion Week and Easter

The season of Lent ends with the entrance of our Lord into Jerusalem and the triumphant procession of Palm Sunday. Nothing from the Old Testament is more appropriate on this day than the promise of Zech. 9:9–10, but the entrance liturgy of the Ark in Ps. 24, with its preceding *torah,* is also fitting as is the story of the bringing of the Ark to Jerusalem in II Sam. 6:1–15.

There follows Maundy Thursday, with the Last Supper and the institution of the new covenant. Jeremiah 31:31–34 comes first to mind, but the story of the original covenant on Mt. Sinai (Ex., ch. 19, and 24:1–11), or of the covenant founding of the people of God as a twelve-tribe confederation (Josh. 24:1–15, 16–28) could also be used. Hosea's proclamation of the new covenant (Hos. 2:14–23) brings out other motifs. And nothing is so instructive of the meaning of the covenant as Deuteronomy's commentaries on it: Deut. 4:1–14; chs. 5; 7:6–11; and especially chs. 27:9–10 or 29:10–15. That merciful proclamation of Deuteronomy, "This day you have become the people of the LORD your God" (Deut. 27:9), sums up God's forgiveness of us and furnishes the basis for our obedience and gratitude toward him.

Good Friday, the telling of the crucifixion, then makes the covenant a reality, and as the New Testament writers do, it is imperative for the preacher to use the Old Testament on this day to proclaim the significance of Jesus' death. As we saw in Chapter V, the crucifixion is understood by the New Testament writers in terms of the Suffering Servant (Isa. 52:13 to 53:12), as the parallel to the exodus out of Egypt (Ex., ch. 14), with its sacrifice of the Passover lamb (Ex., ch. 12) as the fulfillment of the Levitical sacrificial system with its Day of Atonement (Lev., ch. 16), as the perfect offering of the High Priest after the order of Melchizedek (Ps. 110), and as the suffering of the pious righteous worshiper of the psalms (Ps. 22). The use of any one of these Old Testament texts can deepen the witness to the cross.

But other Old Testament passages also illumine Jesus' death—the conversation of Abraham with Yahweh concerning the effect that the righteous man has in turning aside Yahweh's judgment (Gen. 18:22–33); the story of the sacrifice of Isaac (Gen. 22:1–19), with Abraham's prophetic statement, "God will provide himself the lamb for a burnt offering, my son"; Second Isaiah's references to the new exodus (Isa. 43:14–

137

21; 42:14–17; etc.) and to the fact that it is God who has subjected Israel to punishment (Isa. 42:23 to 43:7; 40:1–2); Jeremiah's lament (Jer. 11:18–20), with its reference to the sheep led to the slaughter, or the lament of Jerusalem (Lam. 1:12–16). Even the psalm of the exodus (Ps. 114) is appropriate to the earthquake and darkness that accompanied the death on the cross.

Many lectionaries do not have suitable readings for Easter from the Old Testament, one of the frequent suggestions being Isa. 25:6–9, because of its reference to the banishment of death in v. 8. But Easter is the victory of God in his Son, and the Old Testament is full of hymns of Yahweh's victory and enthronement as sovereign over all: Ex. 15:1–18, 19–21; Ps. 47; 93; 96; 97; 98; 99; Isa. 52:1–12; 51:9–11. There is the great hymn celebrating God's forgiveness, in Ps. 103, or the individual thanksgivings of Ps. 30 and 118. There is Ezekiel's vision of the resurrection of the dry bones of Israel in Ezek. 37:1–14, and the celebration of Zion in Zeph. 3:14–20. The songs of Israel marvelously set forth the exultation necessary to the people of God at the resurrection, for it was to just such a victory of God that Israel looked forward. To mention two more psalms, what could be more appropriate to Easter than the hymn of Ps. 148 or of Ps. 150? And of course the New Testament's rich use of Ps. 110 to proclaim the Lordship of Christ makes it especially meaningful for the day.

f. Pentecost

Following the Easter season, the creation of the church is remembered on the Day of Pentecost, and the emphasis falls on the gift of the Spirit to the church. Because of the Acts account of Pentecost, Joel 2:28–29 is most often used, and this is quite appropriate, but Num. 11:16–17, 24–30, also forms an analogy to the gift of the Spirit to the church, and Isa. 44:1–5 envisions the time when the Spirit will be poured out on all nations as members of Israel. By way of contrast, Gen. 11:1–9 could serve as the Old Testament lesson for the day, because it pictures the disruption of all community on earth under God's judgment on man's sinful pride; Pentecost marks the answer to Babel then, the time when the unity of mankind is restored, and the fellowship of the church becomes the first-fruit of the final fellowship of the Kingdom.

Pentecost is the beginning of the second portion of the church year, and attention is now centered on the life of the church and the implications of the gospel which has been proclaimed for the people of God. It is during this long season of Pentecost (or in some denominations, of Trinity) that all the facets of the Christian life are to be examined, and the congregation is further to be aided to grow up into the measure of the fullness of Christ. This is the season, therefore, in which the life of the people of God in the Old Testament can serve so powerfully as an analogy to the life of the people of God in Christ. This is the season when Israel's pilgrimage becomes the Christian's journey, and we learn from Israel how to walk in the time between the promise and its fulfillment.

The temptation of the preacher during this season is to preach only topical sermons, and some lectionaries are arranged according to this principle.[12] Further, the temptation is strong to switch the attention from God to man, and the result of both temptations may be a man-centered humanism, a desertion of the Word of God for the words of men. It must be remembered that the Christian life grows out of God's actions alone, and that the basis of all Christian living is always the sacred history. Thus, even when treating various topics, the preacher must proclaim God's working, or he quite literally has nothing Christian to say, and much of his preaching during this season must deepen the congregation's understanding of how it is God deals with them. The following topics consequently come to mind as samples of some of the countless possibilities:

God's holiness—Ex. 19:7–20; Isa. 6:1–12; Hos. 11:1–11; Zech. 14:20–21.

God's forgiveness—Micah 7:18–20; Ps. 32; 51; 130.

God's faithfulness—Gen. 21:1-7; Josh. 21:43-45; 23:14-16; I Kings 8:14-26.

God as Lord of nature—Judg. 6:36-40; I Kings, ch. 18; Isa. 40:12-31.

God's hidden working—Gen., ch. 45; Ex. 2:1-10; Ruth; II Sam., ch. 11; I Kings 19:9-18.

God's work in the affairs of nations—Isa. 10:5-11, 12-19; 45:1-13; ch. 47; Jer., ch. 38; Amos 9:7-8, 9-10; Joel 3:9-16; Ps. 82.

Yahweh alone has the power to save and therefore alone is God—I Kings 18:17-40; Isa., ch. 46; Jer. 10:1-16; Hos., ch. 13.

God's presence—Gen. 28:10-17; Ex. 3:1-12; Josh. 1:1-9; Jer., ch. 1; Ps. 139; Job, ch. 7.

God's sustenance and guidance—Ex., ch. 16; Deut. 1:26-33; II Kings, ch. 4.

God's gift of freedom—Ex. 2:23-25; 3:1-12; Isa. 43:14-21.

God's gift of the family—Gen. 2:18-25; Ps. 128; I Sam., ch. 1.

God's gift of our daily work—Gen. 2:4b-9, 15-17; Ps. 90; 127:1-2.

God's gift of joy—Ps. 4; 37; II Sam. 6:1-15.

God's gift of sanctification—Deut. 30:11-14; Ezek. 36:22-32.

God's gift of abundant life—Deut. 8:1-10; 28:1-14; Ezek. 47:1-12; Ps. 1.

God's gift of his image to man—Gen. 1:26-28; Ps. 8.

The relation of God to the state and politics—I Sam., ch. 8; I Kings, ch. 21; Ps. 72; 146; Isa. 30:1-5; 31:1-5; Micah 3:9-12; Zeph. 3:1-8.

If we keep in mind that the Christian life flows out of the actions of God and forms the response to them, then of course there are almost infinite possibilities of dealing with various aspects of the Christian's life before God, and the following passages are simply samples of a few of the subjects possible:

Worship and prayer—I Kings 8:27-30; Ps. 84; Isa. 1:10-17;

29:13–14; 66:1–4; Jer. 7:1–15; 11:14–17; Hos. 5:15 to 6:6; Amos 5:21–24; Micah 6:6–8; Mal. 1:6–14.

The ministerial office—Jer. 15:15–21; 23:9–12, 13–15, 16–22, 23–32; Ezek. 3:16–21; 13:1–16; Micah 3:5–8; Mal. 2:1–9.

Witness—Ex. 19:1–6; Isa. 43:8–13; Jer. 20:7–12.

The nature of man—Gen. 2:4b–7; 6:5–8; Job, ch. 10; Ps. 39; 90; Isa. 40:6–8.

Trust—Gen. 15:1–6; Ps. 91; 131; 139; 27:1–6; Isa. 30:15–18; 7:1–9; Hab. 2:1–4.

Thanksgiving—Deut. 26:5–11; Ps. 66.

Hope—Micah 7:1–7; Lam. 3:1–33.

The necessity and problem of suffering—Gen., ch. 32; Ps. 73; 123; Job 30:9–31; Jer. 12:1–6; Hab. 1:12 to 2:4; Mal. 3:13–18.

Mercy toward others—Deut. 24:17–22; Jonah 4:6–11.

Giving—I Chron. 29:10–19.

The unity of the church—Ps. 133; Isa. 19:23, 24–25; Ezek. 37:15–28; Zech. 8:20–23.

The Kingdom—Ps. 47; Isa. 65:17–25.

The use of the earth and ecology—Gen. 1:28–31; Ps. 104; Ezek. 33:23–29.

The occult and astrology—Gen. 1:14–19; Ps. 19; 148; Isa. 28:14–22; Jer. 7:16–20; 44:15–30; Ezek. 13:17–23.

The use of power—Deut. 16:18–20; Isa. 14:1–21; Jer. 22:1–9, 13–19; Micah 3:1–4.

Divorce—Mal. 2:13–16.

The problem of being in the world and not of it—I Sam., ch. 13.

The list could go on and on, but perhaps enough examples have been given to suggest how varied is the Old Testament's witness to the nature of life before God and how many are the riches to be mined from it.

Another possibility for the preacher during the Pentecost season is to preach a series of sermons on one book or one passage from the Old Testament. For example, ten sermons on the Decalogue, and the way the Testaments themselves interpret those ancient covenant commands would give the widest-ranging examination of the Christian life. Or the preacher could preach a series of sermons from Genesis or Exodus, from Deuteronomy or one of the prophets. Not only would this familiarize the congregation with the Biblical history but it would also root the proclamation more firmly in the actual history of Israel than is often the case with a topical sermon.

3. Pairing an Old Testament Text with a New

We have presented lectionary possibilities from the Old Testament, but it must be emphasized that no sermon can become the word of God for the Christian church if it deals only with the Old Testament apart from the New. In every sermon rising out of an Old Testament text there must be reference to the New Testament outcome of the Old Testament's word. The questions always in dealing with the Old Testament, as we have said before, are: What happened to these ancient words? Did they come to pass? Were they shown to be real words of God? And it is the New Testament alone that can answer these questions. Consequently, every reading from the Old Testament should be paired with a New Testament lesson, and if the preacher chooses an Old Testament text first, then he must also choose a New Testament text to go with it.

Some denominations prescribe both an Epistle and a Gospel reading, but the practical result of this has been to read Epistle and Gospel and to omit the Old Testament lesson. It would be much better to read the Old Testament and the Epistle *or* Gospel, since just as the Old Testament has no outcome without the New, so also the New has no full presentation of the message of salvation without the Old, as we have shown. The question is, then, On what basis can a New Testament text be paired with an Old, or vice versa?

We have suggested several answers to this question. Let us summarize them:

1. The preacher can choose a New Testament passage that uses the Old Testament text in question, or that shows its historical outcome. When this is the case, the New Testament controls very closely the interpretation of the Old Testament text.

2. The preacher can choose a New Testament passage that has the same motif or theme as is found in the Old Testament text.

3. The preacher can choose a New Testament pericope that contrasts the New Testament outcome with the Old Testament word, but caution should be exercised to make certain there is really a contrast involved. The new life in Christ is much more often a fulfillment of the word of the Old Testament than a contrast to it.

4. Occasionally the preacher may want to use Old Testament passages that simply illumine or deepen the New Testament's witness, but very rarely can the Old Testament be used legitimately merely as a historical background explanation for the New, since the Old Testament is telling not only of the customs and ideas of men but primarily of the actions of God.

5. The preacher can choose a New Testament passage that shows a situation in the life of the church or the individual Christian that is analogous to the life of Israel or an Israelite before God.

The practical question is, of course, How is the preacher to find these passages in the New Testament which can be paired with the Old? It is to be hoped that the preacher who has been in the pastorate a few years will, out of his own study of the Bible, be intimately acquainted with the contents of the New Testament and can make such choices out of the depths of his own knowledge. But to avoid subjectivism and the concentration on a few favorite passages, the preacher also has a valuable tool in those editions of the Bible which are printed with center-column cross-references.[13] These cross-references go beyond the textual footnotes found in the RSV, for example, and list other passages where the same words, themes, and even allusions can be located. In pairing texts, and indeed in plumbing the depths of a text within the Old or New Testament itself, the use of such cross-references is invaluable.

B. PREPARING THE SERMON

1. *Understanding the Text*

The weakness of most preaching rests on the minister's failure to understand fully the content of the Biblical passages with which he purports to deal. Christian clergymen are very busy men, and even the most dedicated and well-intentioned of them will usually study a text until an idea suggests itself for a sermon. At that point, all study stops, the sermon is written, and the depths of the text are never plumbed. The result is that the congregation is usually subjected, not to the proclamation of the Biblical word, but to the idea that the preacher has in the back of his own mind.

Sometimes this is a preconceived idea, having nothing to do with the text. For example, I have often assigned preachers in my classes the task of writing a sermon on the Fourth Commandment, "Remember the sabbath day, to keep it holy . . ." (Ex. 20:8–11), and the inevitable result has been a sermon on the necessity of worship. But the basic thrust of the Fourth Commandment has nothing to do with worship. Instead, it concerns man's work and man's rest from work: God, as the Lord of time, graciously gives to man a day when he can rest from all his labors. God has set aside a period of rest, that is, he has "hallowed it," and man is to observe that which God has set apart (cf. Gen. 2:3). It is principally with this rest from labor, then, that a sermon on the Fourth Commandment should deal.

Sometimes the failure of the preacher fully to understand his

144

text leads to a sermon that may be generally sound and theologically helpful, but is unrelated to the passage read from the Scriptures. For example, consider the following outline of a sermon on Isa. 60:1: "Arise, shine; for your light has come, and the glory of the LORD has risen upon you." [14]

Introduction: We experience a great event every morning—the rising of the sun.
  I. The coming of the Messiah is like the rising of the sun.
      1. It gives light. The world lost its way before Christ came.
      2. It reveals ugliness. We all have our dark cellars of sin which the light reveals.
      3. It gives life. There is no life within us without Christ.
      4. It gives warmth, the love of God for the world.
  II. Arise
      1. The commands in the Old and New Testaments to "rise," "get going."
      2. This is the command to the church today.
      3. But we are often paralyzed:
          a. By our ties to the past.
          b. By our desire to stay in the upper room.
  III. Shine
      1. There are two ways of shining.
          a. Indirect light. We are to be the mirror of Christ and must not block his light with our specks of sin.
          b. Direct light. All light comes from the death of the light giver. We can burn ourselves out the wrong way.
      2. The command to us is to arise, shine, get going.

Such a sermon has a lot of helpful ideas in it, but it is almost totally unrelated to Isa. 60:1–7, the lesson read for the morning. That passage is addressed to Zion-Israel and says nothing directly about the Messiah. The result is that the congregation has heard the theology of the preacher and not the word of

God which is mediated through Trito-Isaiah. The Scripture lesson, which talks about camels and flocks and an altar, remains for the people a passage that they probably have not understood and therefore simply another one of those confusing jumbles of words they are so accustomed to hearing from the Old Testament.

To avoid such errors, the preacher must set as his first task the attempt fully to understand for himself what his Old Testament text is saying. He must ask of each text: What does this text, in its historical and literary and tradition context, actually say to Israel? What was the writer's intention? What were his major points? That the preacher should use all the historical, literary, textual, and critical tools at his disposal to answer these questions goes, I hope, without saying. The main point we would emphasize is that the preacher must listen to the text in its fullness, not ending his study of the passage as soon as a sermon idea presents itself, but analyzing and pondering the whole passage, until all its inner and outer relationships and thrusts become clear. Such an exercise takes time and meditation and wrestling with the text on the part of the preacher, but only if a clergyman engages in it will he adequately prepare himself to mediate the word of God to his people, and, after all, the clergyman has no other reason for his office.

2. Relating the Old Testament to the New

Having established the meaning of the whole passage in itself, the preacher is presented with the second question of how the Old Testament passage is related to the pericope paired with it from the New Testament. In actual practice, it may not be until this stage of sermon preparation that the preacher can adequately choose a New Testament lesson, since not until he fully understands the Old Testament lesson can he join a New Testament passage to it. And obviously he is going to have to bring the same study to the chosen New Testament pericope that he did to the Old. But having accomplished this and paired his texts, the clergyman must then delve deeper into how the texts are related. It is at this stage that all the hermeneutical principles for which we have laid the basis in the previous chapters must be brought into play, for it is at this stage that the clergyman can most grievously misinterpret the Old Testament. Let us illustrate with two examples.[15]

a. Avoiding Developmentalism

We pointed out in Chapter II how the Old Testament was lost in the church through its interpretation from the standpoint of developmentalism. Despite the fact that developmentalism was a phenomenon of Biblical scholarship largely in the first three decades of this century and before, it still forms the method by which many preachers relate the Old and New Testaments. Consider the following outline of a sermon on Ps. 1 and Luke 15:11–32 (the parable of the prodigal son):

Introduction: The setting of the psalm.
    1. Jews under the domination of the Greek empire.
    2. The temptation of adopting Greek culture, without the ethical standards of the Jews.
    3. This psalm is an ancient teacher's warning against this temptation.
  I. Blessed is the man who associates with the right kind of people (Ps. 1:1).
    1. The importance of proper friends and companions for a child.
    2. Our relationships leave their mark on us.
 II. Blessed is the man who fills his mind with things of eternal value (Ps. 1:2).
    1. Our life is built from the material we put into it.
    2. We can fill our mind with trash, or with good literature and music and the Bible.
III. The way of the wicked leads to ruin (Ps. 1:4–5).
IV. But morality is not enough for the Christian: the parable of the prodigal son.

1. The elder son was like the man in Ps. 1, but morality did not make him a Christian.
2. He did all the right things, but in the wrong spirit.
3. We must have love. This is righteousness.
V. The reward of the righteous is to be in the congregation of the righteous.
1. We experience the Father's love.
2. We experience the fellowship of the church.
Conclusion: If religion is simply a matter of morality, it is nothing. It must be a matter of the heart, which then brings blessing.

The presupposition of the writer of this sermon was that Ps. 1 deals only with external, legalistic morals and that the New Testament progresses beyond this understanding to a religion of the heart and love. Because of this developmentalistic presupposition, the writer overlooked the gift of abundant life given to the psalmist in his communion with God, indeed he ignored verse 3 of the psalm altogether, and really made the psalm of no value in the eyes of his congregation. Such preaching does not mediate the word of God; it makes the Old Testament's witness to it unnecessary.

As the corrective of developmentalism, we pointed out that the Old and New Testaments are indissolubly related to one another on the basis of promise and fulfillment. Jesus Christ is the fulfillment of every major tradition history of the Old Testament, and that which is promised by God in the Old Testament is realized and completed and made flesh in the New. Because this is true, we further pointed out that the story of Israel in the Old Testament is analogous to the church's life before God in the New, and indeed forms the pattern for it. The church becomes the new Israel in Christ and, in its own time, "relives" Israel's history of salvation. It is on the basis of both of these facts that the Testaments may be related in preaching.

b. Maintaining the Historical Relation of the Old and New Testaments

As we emphasized before, however, this connection between the Old and the New Testament is a historical connection, and in preparing his sermon, the preacher must always keep this historical foundation clearly in mind. The Scriptures must not be divorced from their history and turned into a set of general moral precepts as in the following sermon on Deut. 29:10–15:

I. We must stand.
    1. Each man is called upon to make a covenant decision.
    2. The time is now—this day.
    3. The decision must be constantly renewed.
    4. Our decision has results.

II. We must stand together.
    1. We are related to those before us, those around us, those after us.
    2. We cannot escape community.
    3. Our decisions affect community.

III. We must stand and decide because we are in the presence of the living God.
    1. God's demands upon us call us to decision.
    2. Jesus' calls to decision:
        a. "No one can serve two masters."
        b. "Every one who acknowledges me before men, I also will acknowledge before my Father who is in heaven."
        c. "He who is not with me is against me."

Such a sermon is totally divorced from its historical context. There is no explanation here as to where the words of the text come from or to what concrete situation they were directed. As a result, such a sermon lays a terrible burden upon the people to whom it is preached. It lays an absolute demand upon them and gives them no resources for meeting that demand. They are not told that the words of the text were originally addressed to the people of God in the seventh century B.C. and that despite all their sin, that people was accepted into covenant relation with its God. They are not told that they are the historical continuation of that people through the sacrifice of Jesus Christ. The entire context of God's gracious action toward his chosen people is removed, and the preacher's congregation is supposed to make a proper decision apart from the context of grace and mercy and forgiveness which is inherent in the covenant relationship. By removing the history of salvation, the preacher has removed all possibility of obedience and faithfulness on the part of his people, for it is God's gracious action in the sacred history alone, mediated to us through the Scripture and worship, that makes possible our response of trust and love and gratitude to God.

Further, by removing this text from its historical context and turning it into a general moral admonition, the preacher has made it unreal. The argument of the congregation in reply to this sermon could very well be: "Why are we in the presence of the living God? You say we are, preacher, but how do we know that? Where and how does God confront us? And what responsibility do we have to make a decision for or against him?" Once again, only if the preacher has set the text in its concrete historical setting can these questions be answered. God confronted Israel, according to Deuteronomy, in the ceremony of covenant renewal, and he confronts us similarly in the ceremony of covenant renewal which we know as the Lord's Supper, and both ceremonies spring out of a history of salvation which has taken place and through which God has entered into relation with his people. But without that history, there is no confrontation of God with his people, and there is no basis for claiming that there is. It is the history, the actions of God, upon which every sermon must be based, or it has no basis at all.

3. Relating the Text to the Congregation

This necessity for emphasizing the historical content of the text leads to the further consideration, in preparing his sermon, of how the preacher is to relate his texts from the Old and New Testaments to the congregation in front of him. The question is, How can we legitimately jump from the "then" of the texts to the "now" of the congregation? This is the heart of the hermeneutical problem, and we have suggested that its answer lies partly in the fact that the present-day church is the historical continuation in faith of the covenant people of God. The ancient words of the Bible are the mediators of the word of God to us, because they were addressed to God's chosen people and we have now become that people through our faith in the person and work of Jesus Christ. In other words, the word of God deals with Israel, which is the people of God, and only if we have become the new Israel in Christ is there the possibility of the Bible speaking to us as the word of God.

a. A Similar Human Situation?

It follows then that any sermon which ignores or dissolves the relation of the text to Israel is going to go astray, and this is a common error in all those sermons which attempt to relate the Old Testament to the present church on the basis of a similar *human* situation. Consider the following sermon on Josh. 24:15-16,[16] "Choose this day whom you will serve, . . . but as for me and my house, we will serve the LORD":

Introduction: These words were spoken by Joshua to desert nomads who had entered the Promised Land. Could they now withstand the perils of prosperity?
    1. This is a question to us Americans. We were once pioneers, and now have prosperity and plenty.
    2. This presents us with a moral imperative. The good life does not follow automatically.
  I. We must choose because we have but one life to live, and that a short one.
    1. We cannot experience everything.
    2. Surrounded by luxuries, we are tempted to try.
  II. We must choose because abundant living comes by decision and discipline.
  III. We must choose because we carry almost unlimited possibilities within us.

IV. We must choose, because if we do not choose, our choices will be made for us.
   1. Without purpose, we have only conformity.
   2. I pray you choose God, whose will is your peace and in whose service is perfect freedom. (One sentence.)

The crucial point at which this sermon erred was its identification of Israel with Americans in general, on the basis of a "similar" pioneer past and settlement into a new and prosperous land. At that point, Israel, the people who had been brought into relation with God through the long history which Josh. 24:2–13 very carefully recites, was dissolved into a group of people similar to any group of emigrants to a new land. In short, Israel's and therefore our relation to God dropped out of the picture. The text ceased to be a mediator of the word of God to his people and became a general moral admonition to all Americans to make decisions. Not surprisingly, reference to the Lord was introduced again only in the last sentence of the sermon.

This is vivid illustration of the fact that once the character of Israel as the covenant people of God is ignored, the words of the Old Testament lose their force as the word of God and become for us no more important than any other moral directive, from whatever source. A sermon from an Old Testament text must not dissolve the connection of the text with the historical people of God. Otherwise the text ceases to be a channel for the word of God and becomes only a word of man.

b. A Common Humanity?

The foregoing comments apply equally to those sermons which attempt to relate the Old Testament to the modern congregation on the basis of a common humanity, a device that is most often found in sermons from The Psalms. Because so many of the psalms record the spiritual experiences and insights of worshipers, with little concrete reference to history or to Israel, the temptation of many preachers is to turn the psalms into expressions of experiences common to mankind as a whole. Indeed, such a device for interpreting the psalms is used by H. H. Rowley,[17] C. S. Lewis,[18] and T. H. Robinson. In his 1947 book *Poetry and Poets of the Old Testament,* the latter says of the Psalter: "What really matters about the book is that it mirrors thoughts and feelings which are common to all ages in history. Human nature is still human nature, and human needs recur age after age." [19]

Beyond the question of whether human nature and needs remain the same from age to age and culture to culture—a highly problematical statement—the fact is that the Psalter is the product of Israel. Its piety grows out of the worship of a people who have been redeemed by God, given a covenant and land and king, and then judged for their unfaithfulness and sent into exile, and not one of the psalms can properly be understood apart from that context. And only if we through faith share in Israel's history before God, as the new Israel in Christ, can we pray her prayers, and weep with her in her laments, and rejoice with her in her thanksgivings. Otherwise we do not know the God to whom she prays, and her prayers and celebrations are not possible to us.

c. Avoiding Allegory

Another temptation that often besets the preacher who is trying to relate his text to the modern congregation is the temptation to lose the history of the Old Testament by allegorizing it. So many of the experiences and words and institutions of Israel seem so long ago and far away, totally divorced from the life of the twentieth century and having no relevance for space-age men, and when the preacher finds himself confronted by what seems to be an antiquated text, he escapes the problems involved by making the text stand for something other than its original historical reference. For example, in his exposition in *The Interpreter's Bible* on the story of Joseph, the late Walter Russell Bowie takes Gen. 37:24 and turns it into an allegory on the state of the human soul:

Joseph is thrown by his brothers into a pit—a dreadful physical fact. But morally and spiritually, too, it may often seem that the soul of man is in a pit.[20]

This allegory is then developed into a full-blown exposition of the way in which the soul of humanity may "seem to be in a pit." To be sure, the exposition is imaginatively done, drawing lessons out of the story of Joseph which are then applied to the condition of humanity. But the end result is that the real history of the Old Testament is lost, and with it the saving action of God. The members of the modern congregation, who are so used to allegories and moralisms and ethical admonitions preached to them from the Old Testament—when the Old Testament is preached at all—must instead hear proclaimed the story of God's actions in Israel's history, for it is on the basis of those actions alone, finally completed in Jesus Christ, that their salvation has come and they have been redeemed from evil and death.

d. Symbolism and History

There are, to be sure, some passages in the Old Testament, as in the New, in which a deliberate symbolism is employed, and the preacher has not abandoned history or fallen into allegorizing when he continues such symbolism. For example, to use another illustration from *The Interpreter's Bible,*[21] in commenting on Num. 2:2, Albert George Butzer applies the text to the need to put the church back again at the center of the community's life. The text reads as follows:

The people of Israel shall encamp each by his own standard, with the ensigns of their fathers' houses; they shall encamp facing the tent of meeting on every side.

Butzer's application of the text is debatable on the ground that it is a far cry from the ancient Israelite tent of meeting to the modern church, and the two cannot immediately be related. On the other hand, the deliberate symbolism of the Numbers text is of God in the midst of his people, if only in occasional descents to the tent, and insofar as God is present in his church also through the Word and Sacraments, Butzer's application of the text to the church can be defended. But perhaps Butzer's exposition of this text illustrates the problems involved in making the hermeneutical jump from the "then" of the text to the "now" of the modern congregation.

More clear-cut are the uses of symbolism in Second Isaiah, to cite another example. The prophet uses many figures in his oracles to portray Israel's situation of separation from God—the figure of the wilderness (Isa. 40:3; 41:18–19; 43:19–20; 51:3) and thirst (Isa. 41:17; 55:1; cf. ch. 44:3), of warfare (Isa. 40:2) and imprisonment (Isa. 42:7, 22; 49:9), of blindness (Isa. 42:7, 16, 18–20; 43:8) and deafness (Isa. 42:18–19; 43:8)—and such symbolism may therefore legitimately be used in preaching from these texts. Nevertheless, it must be remembered that these figures are applied to *Israel's* situation in the sixth century B.C. The texts are not talking about mankind in general, but about the people of God. It is they who are blind and deaf and in prison and thirsting in the wilderness. And it is within that covenant context that the texts must be used.

To make the latter point clear, let me cite another example. I recently wrote a Bible study on Hosea for the Lutheran Church Women.[22] In commenting on Hos. 1:8–9, I stated: "Yahweh now announces that his relationship with Israel is broken. . . . Israel now will be without God in the world." Unfortunately, the editor of this Bible study series added to this comment: "There are millions in our world today who are without God. The words of Hosea are not only for the past." [23] By adding these words, the editor of the series entirely missed the point of Hos. 1:8–9. The text does not deal with all those millions in the world who are without God or who have never heard of Yahweh of Israel. The text deals with Israel herself, and the announcement of the text is that Yahweh abandons his people and declares his covenant with her at an end. By turning words addressed to Israel into words addressed to mankind in general, the editor changed the whole meaning of Hosea's announcement, and it is such changes and such distortions of the text—brought about by abandoning the historical content of the text—which we must strenuously avoid in our preaching. We hear the word of God from the Bible through the mediation of his specifically chosen historical people or we do not hear it at all. The preacher must, above all else, cling to the salvation history in the Scriptures.

e. Involvement with the Text

There is another common error to which preachers fall victim when they prepare a sermon on an Old Testament text, and this is the error of talking *about* the text rather than proclaiming it. Once again this is a shortcoming frequently found in sermons from The Psalms, although it crops up in relation to other texts as well. Consider the following expository sermon on Ps. 98:

I. The theme of the psalm: sing a new song.
    1. Arises with fresh enthusiasm from a new appreciation of God's goodness.
    2. Because God has performed great deeds for Israel.
II. The psalmist speaks from the certainty of the knowledge of God and his strength.
    1. No doubts blur his concentration on God as central to all creation.
    2. All the earth will know and feel the impact of God's greatness.
    3. The emphasis is thanksgiving and praise, because God is at the center.
III. The psalmist urges all creation to join in the praise.
    1. The tumult of Israel's worship.
    2. Because God was with them.
IV. God comes in judgment.
    1. Is greeted with rejoicing by Israel.
    2. Because God is righteous.
V. We can translate this into the experience of the Christian community.
    1. Our great hymns.

2. There is a joy deeper than sorrow. Christ sang on the way to the cross (Heb. 12:2—"For the joy that was set before him, he endured the cross").
3. In this, we can find the courage to sing. (One sentence.)

The major difficulty with this sermon is that it merely describes the content of the psalm. The worshipers are led, verse by verse through the psalm, to stand back and look at the psalmist's joy. They are spectators to the psalm's celebration, but are given no reason for entering into it, except in one sentence at the end of the sermon. The result is that the psalm remains really a matter of indifference to the congregation and certainly no call to praise. The members of the congregation will go home after the sermon in much the same state as when they entered the church.

This is illustrative of the fact that the purpose of the sermon is to make the words of the text the words also of the listening congregation. When the cry goes out, "O sing to the Lord a new song, for he has done marvelous things!" that cry must immediately be grounded in the actual action of God toward the congregation. The preacher must immediately ask, On what basis can we sing a new song to the Lord? And immediately the presence of Christ in his congregation and his working among them comes to the fore. They have just received Christ's forgiveness in the assurance of pardon in the liturgy, or they will soon receive the gift of new life in the celebration of the Supper, or they have just entered into the events of the crucifixion or resurrection through the reading of the Scripture. Again, perhaps the worshipers have experienced some particular renewal of their life, for which they want to thank God, or perhaps one of the members has been delivered from death, or maybe the generosity of the congregation, inspired by Christ's spirit of service, has overflowed in a special gift. Then on the basis of God's actual working among them through Christ, the congregation can enter into the praises of

157

this psalm and sing a new song to the Lord for the marvelous things he has done and the victory he has wrought.

The point is that this psalm, and the Bible as a whole, proclaims the actions of God, and the task of the sermon is to present that action and to allow the congregation to participate in it. We are not spectators of the salvation history, but participants in it, and Israel in the Old Testament is not a strange people to be observed, but the congregation of God of which we also have become members through Christ. Thus the words of the Old Testament text, spoken to Israel, must be shown to be words spoken to us also, and the praises and laments of Israel in The Psalms and cultic proclamations must be made our possessions. If the sermon accomplishes these goals, it then may become a channel for the word of God.

f. Translating the Biblical Language for the Congregation

If the words of the Bible are to become media of the word of God for us, it is quite clear that they must be made comprehensible. With the widespread ignorance of the Scriptures in our congregations and the secularity of our times, there is much in the Bible that the modern congregation is not going to understand, and the preacher must constantly and consciously teach his congregation in his sermon the meaning of the Biblical language.

We cannot even assume these days that everyone in the congregation understands who we mean when we say the word "God." Many will think of a sentimental little godlet of tender feeling or of a mystical presence in nature or of an ethical ideal, and rarely of Yahweh of Israel. Or when we use the word "sin," the automatic translation of the term for some in the congregation will be "sex" or "moral debauchery," but they will seldom apply the term to their own pride or unfaithfulness in decision-making. These things have to be explained and of course, as we have pointed out, the proclamation of the gospel has to include, first of all, the witness to who God is, as he is revealed in Israel and finally in Jesus Christ. Out of the knowledge of God, all else follows, as Hosea and Jeremiah made so clear.

Further, there are certainly basic terms in the Biblical language which must once again be filled with content for the modern congregation. Few of our people know the Biblical significance of the word "redeemer"—that it is a "buying back" of a family member who has fallen into slavery. Few know what the "covenant" was, or what "salvation" means in Biblical terms, or how the Bible views God's "judgment." The sermon must elucidate these terms and not take for granted their comprehensibility to the congregation.

But beyond this didactic function of the preacher, there is his function as the translator and modernizer of the Biblical language. There is much in the Bible that is couched in the terms of the ancients' world view, the most prominent being perhaps the Bible's view of a three-story universe, with its heavens and firmament, and flat earth and pillars anchored in the sea, and chaos and Sheol and evil darkness. These permeate the Biblical record, and to ask the modern congregation to view their universe in such terms is to ask the impossible of them: that they cease to be twentieth-century human beings and return to the world view of the ancient Near East.

Nevertheless, in preparing his sermon and dealing with his text, the preacher must cling to the witness to God which is mediated through such an ancient world view. For example, Gen., ch. 1, shares all the features of the ancients' view of the universe, but proclaimed through that view is the basic Hebrew witness to God's relation to his creation. He is transcendent sovereign over his world, not bound up or contained in its life and therefore not transitory or dying or revealed through nature's round. He deals with his creation solely through the medium of his word, and remains uniquely other than all things and persons he has made. We would not express his transcendence in modern language by saying he is enthroned in the heaven of heavens above the smooth arc of the firmament, and we would not give witness to his sovereignty by saying he has conquered the chaos dragon. But if as we discard the Biblical language we discard the Old Testament's witness to God's sovereign transcendence over his creation, then we will basically distort the Biblical witness to God and make it impossible for our congregations to understand who God really is. The archaic language of the text must be explained and elucidated and translated, but the witness of the text must remain and the meaning of the text must be brought home to the modern worshiper.

C. THE MIRACLE OF PREACHING

There is a miracle that takes place in preaching. It does not occur every Sunday morning, no matter how skilled the preacher, and it cannot be produced by any wiles or will of man. Rather, it occurs when God wills it, and it is solely the product of his working. It is the miracle whereby the words proclaimed from the pulpit become the word of God for the congregation, the miracle of God's use of human language to reveal himself to his worshipers.

This miracle is of the most active and effective nature, for it is the nature of the word of God that it always creates a new situation. This fact is seen very clearly in the witness of the Scriptures to the word. God's word effects the creation of the world; God says, "Let there be light," and there is light (Gen. 1:3), a witness with which we all are familiar (cf. Ps. 33:6, 9). But the Scriptures are equally certain that God's word also creates and acts within history. In the words of Second Isaiah, God sends forth his word and it does not return to him empty, but it accomplishes that which he purposes and prospers in the thing for which he sent it (Isa. 55:11). For Ezekiel, the word which Yahweh speaks is performed (Ezek. 12:28), and for Jeremiah it cannot be held back (Jer. 20:9). It "runs swiftly" to accomplish God's purpose on earth (Ps. 147:15), and it "lights upon" Israel, in Isaiah, bringing to pass within her life that which God intends (Isa. 9:8).

160

So too is the case when the words of a Biblical passage or of a sermon become the word of God for a congregation. Then a new situation is created, and the word accomplishes that of which it speaks. The worshipers do not merely hear about judgment; they are in fact judged—set into that situation of separation from God which calls their entire existence into question. Or if the people hear a sermon that becomes God's word of forgiveness to them, they are in fact brought back into a new communion of life with their Lord. Or if they hear the Biblical story of redemption, and God reveals himself through that story, then the listening people are really released from their slavery of the past and given a new freedom to act as God's sons. The word of God, spoken through the Bible or the sermon, acted out or remembered in the liturgy, creates within God's receptive people the situation of which it speaks. God very definitely, through the action of his word, makes all things new. The word acts; it is effective force. But it is given only by God. Our human words become God's word only when he in his sovereignty so decides it.

There is a very real sense, then, in which we preachers merely "prepare the way of the LORD." God in his wisdom chose the witness of Israel and the witness to Jesus Christ as the means for revealing himself to all the families of the earth. And we preachers are called upon to make that witness clear. We are called upon to tell the Biblical story as simply and as effectively as possible. We are called upon to communicate the message of the Bible.

By avoiding hermeneutical errors such as those we have discussed in this chapter, we enable our congregations to hear the Biblical word. We remove the obstacles that stand in the way of understanding the text, and we let the Bible have its say. We allow the Scriptures to proclaim their message to our congregations.

Moreover, it is possible for us preachers to use homiletical methods that will drill the Biblical text into the consciousness of our hearers. By the use of vivid and gripping language, by the employment of illustrations and rhythmic language and

161

timing in delivery, even by the use of appropriate gestures and proper lighting and effective speaking voice, a preacher can do much to open the ears of his congregation or to close them. When one hears a pedantic preacher, one is sometimes tempted to think that the worst sin in preaching is that of boring a congregation! As my former homiletics teacher, Paul Scherer, once put it, "I can teach a man to write an English sentence and to prepare a sermon outline, but I cannot give him the fire." There is preaching that is afire, and there is preaching that faintly sputters, and the difference lies partly in the vividness with which the preacher writes, the sense of timing and drama with which he speaks, and the sincerity and zeal which he brings to his task.

That is all human skill, however, and some of it can be taught. But Scherer's words point even more to the fact that the most accomplished of writers and orators cannot turn his human words into the word of God. The preacher removes the obstacles to hearing the text; he proclaims it and interprets it for his people to the best of his homiletical ability. But then every preacher must wait for God to come and to use his human words as the channel of his divine working. We preachers prepare the way of the Lord. We smooth out the road and get rid of the stumbling blocks. We announce the coming of God. And then we simply wait. As the psalmist bids Israel do, we "wait for the LORD." We wait for him to make our words the media of his word.

That God so uses our words is the miracle of preaching. But use them he does to work his will in his church and his world. Sometimes through our faithfulness, oftentimes in spite of us, God pours the treasures of his self-revelation into the earthen vessels of our preaching. Indeed, he tells us through the apostle Paul that men will not know him without a preacher. And we are thus called to be the mediators of the living God to our fellowmen. Never was so awesome a task entrusted to men and women. Never was so glorious a calling given as that given to us, his proclaimers.

CHAPTER VII

Valid Method
and Some Sample Sermons

LET US SUMMARIZE the thesis of this book. The valid use of the Old Testament in the Christian pulpit is built upon the historical fact that Jesus Christ, as proclaimed in the New Testament, is the completion and fulfillment of the word of God witnessed to in the Old Testament. On this basis, the Old Testament is given to the Christian as the promise of Jesus Christ, not just in its prophetic portions but as a whole. Jesus Christ is the final reinterpretation of every major tradition in the Old Testament, and Jesus Christ is therefore fully proclaimed only when the Old Testament portion of his story is also proclaimed.

According to the New Testament, because Jesus Christ is the completion of the Old Testament salvation histories, the people of Jesus Christ are also the final shape of the people of God toward which Yahweh works in the Old Testament. The church becomes through its Lord the inheritor of the promises to Israel and, as the prophets had foreseen, the church "relives" the history of Israel. Its life before its God becomes analogous to the life of the old Israel, and Israel's story therefore serves the church as instruction and warning and guide. Israel's story becomes for the church revelatory of its own situation of pilgrimage.

It is these two fundamental hermeneutical facts, born out of the witness of the Scriptures, upon which all valid preaching from the Old Testament can and must be based. As we saw in the previous chapter, preaching from the Old Testament cannot properly rest upon developmentalism, upon moralism, upon allegory. The Old Testament is not given to the Christian as revelatory of a similar human situation or of a common humanity. It holds no interest for the Christian as simply an antiquated documentary of man's former religious experience. The Old Testament is given to the Christian only as the promise of Jesus Christ and as the story of what the church has become through its faith in Jesus Christ.

This does not mean that the Christian preacher and congregation are to read Jesus Christ back into the Old Testament. At every point, the Christian must cling to the actual history witnessed to in the Old Testament, for it is precisely that history which finally culminates in the Word made flesh and the birth of the Christian church. If the history is lost, the fulfillment in Jesus Christ is lost, and our Lord and his church become totally inexplicable. The Scriptures are the testimony to what God has actually done, and if the actions of God in Israel and his Son Jesus are reduced to ideas or symbols or "eternal truths," there is no basis for our faith. To paraphrase the words of Paul, if the holy history has not taken place, then "our preaching is in vain," our "faith is futile," we are still in our sins, and "we are of all men most to be pitied" (I Cor. 15:14, 17, 19). In every sermon, the Scriptures' history must be evident, or there is nothing to proclaim.

Our final task, then, is to illustrate in a number of sermons some of the possibilities of preaching from the Old Testament, in relation to the New. Let me emphasize that these sermons are only illustrative. Any one of the texts could have been treated in a different and, I am sure, more effective manner. The content of these sermons is not intended as a model of great preaching. But I am convinced that the method of these sermons is based on sound hermeneutics, and this method will be pointed out in relation to each presentation.

These sermons are not theoretical illustrations; they were preached before actual congregations. Thus their style is not that of the written, but of the spoken, word, and each sermon is prefaced by a notice of the occasion on which it was preached. Some of the illustrative material in the sermons has been updated for the purposes of this book. Otherwise the sermons are presented exactly as they were delivered.

A. THE METHOD OF ANALOGY

This sermon was preached during a Christmas Communion service in the First United Church of Christ, Reading, Pennsylvania. It is illustrative of the use of analogy to link the Old and New Testaments, in that it focuses on the babes given both to Ahaz and to us in support of the promise. The historical context and content of the text are emphasized in carrying through this analogy. Further, the sermon picks up the motif of the "sign" in both Testaments and examines it. And finally, the congregation is involved with the Isaiah passage by the use of quotations from it to speak directly to the people. The words addressed to Ahaz are seen to be words addressed to us, although this is put into a positive rather than a negative form at the end of the sermon.

"And This Shall Be a Sign Unto You"

Scripture Lessons: Isaiah 7:1–17; Luke 2:1–20

"Behold, a young woman shall conceive and bear a son, and shall call his name Immanuel." We all are familiar with the words of this text from the prophecies of Isaiah. And for years, simple Christian believers have taken these words as a prediction of the birth of Jesus Christ. Originally, however, in the Old Testament, these words were not intended that way at all. Rather, they were intended by the prophet Isaiah to be a sign, a proof, to a disbelieving Judean king named Ahaz. Ahaz was in a very tough spot. The year was 734 B.C., and after a century of relative quiet, the monstrous giant of the Assyrian empire had begun to threaten the tiny independent countries of the Near East again. A century earlier, the little states had managed to turn back the giant by joining together in a military coalition against him. And that was exactly what Syria and Northern Israel wanted to do this time too. But Ahaz of Judah refused to go along. He wanted nothing to do with the Northern Israelite king, who had gained the throne by murder. He was quite content to be an isolationist and to avoid international gambles. As a result, Syria and Northern Israel decided to overthrow the government of Ahaz and to put a vassal king on the southern throne. They gathered together their armies, and closed in on Jerusalem.

That meant that Ahaz had two choices. Either he could call the Assyrian army in to his aid or he could rely on God to protect him and his kingdom. You see, Ahaz was a Davidic king, a descendant of the house of David, and God had promised David that his dynasty would never fall. According to the promise, God would protect Jerusalem and its Davidic king. But the question was, Could Ahaz trust anything so flimsy as a promise of God, when he had an enemy army laying siege to Jerusalem?

The point of our Old Testament lesson this morning is that the prophet Isaiah assures Ahaz that he can trust God's word. If you simply cling to God's promise, Isaiah tells the king, God will protect you and will defeat these two enemies who have come up against you. However, if you do not trust God, then you are completely lost. In Isaiah's words: "If you will not believe, surely you shall not be established."

Moreover, says Isaiah, God will give you a sign, a proof, that you can rely on his promise. Somewhere in Judah a young woman will give birth to a son and call his name Immanuel. And that will be the sign that God will keep his word. Scholars think that probably the young woman indicated was the wife either of the prophet or of the king himself. At any rate, Isaiah's words probably came to pass. In 734 the child was born, and in gratitude for her son the young mother named him Immanuel, "God with us." And the child served as God's chosen sign that the Lord would keep his promise.

Now, we have these signs, these proofs of God's working, mentioned all through the Bible. The wonders that Moses and Aaron work are understood as signs to the Egyptian Pharaoh. Jesus' miracles, according to the Gospel of John, are signs that manifest his glory. In Mark and in Matthew, it is said that there will be signs in heaven and on earth at the return of the Son of Man. And in Luke's Christmas story of the shepherds, which we read every year at this time, we hear that God gives a sign that the Savior of the world has been born. "To you is born this day in the city of David a Savior, who is Christ the Lord. And this will be a sign for you: you will find a babe wrapped in swaddling cloths and lying in a manger." Just as for Ahaz in the days of Isaiah, the sign that is given us is the birth of a little child, and this is to serve as proof to us, as it did for Ahaz, that God will send his salvation.

The difficulty with these signs of the Bible is that they don't prove anything. They are easily acceptable, I suppose, by the person who already believes. But how could the birth of a child prove to Ahaz that God was going to rescue him? There were lots of baby boys born in Judah that year, and any pious mother could have named her child Immanuel. In fact, lots of them probably did. What good could a baby with a special name do Ahaz? He certainly didn't need a baby then. Ahaz needed an army!

That is exactly the way we feel about the sign that is given us—about the child wrapped in swaddling clothes and lying in a manger. He's no proof at all that God will rescue you and me, and we don't need a baby for Christmas. We need something we can count on!—something that gives us an iron-clad guarantee that we're going to make it past tomorrow, someone who assures us that this time of ours really does have a happy ending, and that it's not just all going to end with a bang, or, what is worse, with a whimper. Give us a real sign, God—some real life insurance. A baby lying in a manger is no sign at all.

167

You know, if you really stand back and look objectively at Christmas, it can become a pretty hollow affair. One writer that I know put it very vividly: "Time goes to work on Christmas. The myths begin to fall apart; quickly or slowly reality demands its due. Visions of sugarplums turn to hard stares at selfishness, commercialization, bad taste, insincerity, pretense. The fall from innocence splatters itself all over Christmas, dimming the lights on the tree, dirtying the snow. Underneath all the pretty surfaces lie the same old facts of life: it is winter, the trees are bare, the days are short, people are nothing but people, Christ is a plaster doll." [1]

No, the baby lying in the manger is no sign at all—no guarantee for us that we have a Savior. And you and I need a clearer sign that God is at work in this world, a better proof that our life has a meaning and a divine purpose after all.

The frustrating part about it is that we are given no other sign—no other sign of God's work among us—than that babe in a manger. Heaven knows, the men of Jesus' time tried to wrest some other proof from him. Their requests came thick and fast: "Teacher," the scribes and Pharisees said to him, "we wish to see a sign from you" (Matt. 12:38). Or, "If you are the Son of God, command these stones to become loaves of bread." (Matt. 4:3.) Always the question, "Are you he who is to come, or shall we look for another?" (Matt. 11:3). "If you are the King of the Jews, save yourself!" (Luke 23:37.) "Let the Christ, the King of Israel, come down now from the cross, that we may see and believe." (Mark 15:32.) And to it all, the man from Nazareth replied: "Why does this generation seek a sign? Truly, I say to you, no sign shall be given" (Mark 8:12).

There was no absolutely convincing miracle worked, no triumphant descent from the cross, no mighty display that would convince everyone that Jesus was the Savior. If there had been, then everyone would have accepted our Lord, and he would not have been crucified. But instead, there was only a humble carpenter's son, who once had been a babe in a manger. And men looked at him and wondered, and pondered

168

the things that he did. And Jesus turned their questions back to them, "But who do you say that I am?"

It is the manner of the God of the Bible to carry on his work in this world in deep hiddenness. The Hollywood film producers think that when God speaks to man, there are always violins playing heavenly music in the background. Or we think the presence of God is always signaled by an overwhelming spiritual experience. And we do look for miracles. We pray and we pray. And we look for those who are deathly ill suddenly to be healed. We look for homes torn with argument miraculously to become tranquil. We look for a world at war mysteriously to have peace. And yes, we even expect our selfish souls to be comforted and blessed here this morning. There should be certain evidence of his action, if God is at work in this world.

But the God of the Bible does not meet our expectations. He hides himself and seldom gives us the convincing sign that we seek. When he works, it is not in the expected way—not in the gift of healing and peace and tranquillity, but in the very midst of suffering and war and death. In the exile and destruction of the people Israel, and finally in a criminal's cross—that is where the Bible claims that God is most truly present—and instead of comfort and blessing, you and I are challenged this morning to undergo a crucifixion.

God hides himself, and when he comes to us, it is not in the form of a blinding vision, but in the everyday objects of bread and wine. And midst all the turmoil and trouble of our unsettled world, we are given nothing more visible, really, than a cup standing on an altar and a group of people sharing bread.

And all this hiddenness is gathered up in the story of Christmas, and represented for our searching eyes by the figure of a babe in a manger. If ever God's presence among us could be overlooked, it is in that swaddled babe. For what do you have? You have the pain of childbirth in the most forbidding circumstances: a cold night wind blowing outside a stable cave at Bethlehem; an anxious husband tending the birth of a son that is not even his, a little guilty because he could not afford a bribe for an innkeeper's room; the dust of straw, and the smell of animals, and the blood of the afterbirth; and a group of ragged shepherds showing up in the frigid light of the dawn. There is nothing about that scene which could convince anyone that the Savior of the world was present. God hides himself behind blood and flesh, and gives us no certain sign. His redeeming work among us is veiled in weakness and poverty and pain.

That means finally that we are left with nothing more certain at this Christmas season than our very uncertain faith. Like Ahaz in the days of Isaiah, we are given nothing more than a babe, and apparently our whole future depends on whether or not we believe the promise connected with that child.

> If you will not believe,
> surely you shall not be established.

Our life or death, the Scripture says, depends on our trust. And the most important question, then, is, What are we to trust? What is it that we are to believe when we have no other certainty, when no infallible proof has been given that God is at work among us?

We are to believe that nevertheless our Savior has come, and that this holy season remembers his entrance into our lives.

> To you is born this day in the city of David a Savior, who is Christ the Lord.

That is the proclamation that is given to us, the good news that is announced, that our Savior has truly come. And it is that joyful proclamation to which we are to cling. It is that fantastic, marvelous news that we are to believe.

But faith means much more than merely intellectual assent. I suppose most of us here in this church this morning theoretically accept the Christmas message. But faith means really to see Jesus of Nazareth as our Savior, and therefore to value finally only those things which he brings.

170

We pile up a marvelous mound of goods at Christmastime. With all our church and holiday bazaars, our shopping, and our Christmas giving, we store up for ourselves luxury and wealth unequaled by any other people. And let's be frank about it, friends. We enjoy it a great deal. We revel in the gorgeous presents, the juicy turkey, the warmth and comfort of our homes. It is good to be well off and comfortable and snug at Christmastime.

But faith that our Savior has come means to hold it all very lightly, to be willing to give it all up for the things that Christ brings—to be willing to spend and give up wealth for the sake of justice among men, to be able to sacrifice pride and status in exchange for the gift of humility, to be willing to forget self in order to forgive our fellows. With Paul, to have faith is to be willing to count all things as loss for the sake of gaining Christ. And the Scripture says, "If you will not believe, surely you shall not be established."

More than that, certainly we are to trust that it is the Savior alone who brings us the gift of life, and all our efforts to make our own security are inadequate and passing measures. Back there in the days of Isaiah, Ahaz scrambled frantically about to secure himself and his people. An army was massing itself before his capital, and he needed weapons to defend his kingdom. We face the same kind of life-and-death threat in our atomic age, and we scramble frantically through the political and economic world to defend our lives and holdings. But surely the fact that our Savior is born means that no matter what our defenses, we finally will have the gift of life only from his hands. If the stock market collapses, if the world blows up, if our whole way of life is lost, there is finally only one who can hold us secure in his everlasting arms. And to have faith means to affirm that is so—in every decision we make. "If you will not believe, surely you shall not be established."

We have no certain signs given us by God in this uncertain world. We must walk by the faith that our Savior has nevertheless been born. And that means in everything to trust his way with our lives. And where does he lead us? Very often through the valley of the shadow, very often down a path that ends on Golgotha, and we suffer pain in our bodies, and anguish in our homes, and chaos in our society. And very often, all about us, there is nothing but distress and gloom. In the words of Isaiah, "we look to the earth, but behold, distress and darkness, the gloom of anguish; and we are thrust into thick darkness."

But there is good news nevertheless. There is light in the midst of the darkness:

Be not afraid; for behold, I bring you good news of a great joy which will come to all the people; for to you is born this day in the city of David a Savior, who is Christ the Lord. And this will be a sign for you: you will find a babe wrapped in swaddling cloths and lying in a manger. (Luke 2:10–12.)

If you do believe, surely you shall be established.

Amen.

B. THE METHOD OF PROMISE AND FULFILLMENT

This sermon was preached in the Schwab Auditorium of Pennsylvania State University before an academic congregation. It attempts to examine the meaning for a Christian congregation of the ancient promise to Abraham, and it does so by understanding Jesus Christ as the fulfillment of that promise, and indeed as the fulfillment of Abraham's function and faith. Once again the historical context and content of the Genesis narratives are carefully preserved.

THE DECISION ABOUT THE JEW

Scripture Lessons: Genesis, ch. 12; Galatians 3:1–14

"The LORD said to Abram, . . . 'I will bless those who bless you, and him who curses you I will curse; and by you all the families of the earth shall bless themselves.'"

This text from the promise of God to Abraham is surely one

172

of the most offensive passages in all of the Bible. If it is true, if it really is the word of God, it means that you and I have no possibility of life unless we take a positive attitude toward an eighteenth-century B.C. Semite and his descendants.

Yahweh says, "I will bless those who bless you." The meaning is, "I will bless those who consider you to be blessed," and let us be quite clear about just what is involved when God blesses us. We are not dealing here with the Lord's sentimental wish for our happiness. In the Old Testament, "God bless you" is not just a convenient phrase that one can use to wrap up a television show. It is not a pious way for one friend to say good-by to another. It is not even the signal that the Sunday worship service is over, and it certainly is not the tool for an evangelistic crusade, not even if it's phrased, "May the Lord bless you real good." God's blessing of us, in the Bible's usage, is God's gift of power and vitality; it is God pouring out all his strength and goodness on us, so that we have the freedom and well-being to live and to live abundantly. God's blessing is the gift of life. In his typical concreteness, the Hebrew said it brought fertile fields and healthy children and hearts overrunning with joy. And he was quite sure that apart from God's blessing, there were only distress and sterility and death.

So you see our text is talking about life and death, and it makes the terribly offensive statement that we cannot really live unless we consider Abraham and the Israelites to be those people upon whom God has poured out his life and strength and favor. Either we see God at work in Abraham and his people or we die. That's what our text is saying. And we do not like the decision that such a text makes necessary.

We do need the promised blessing, however. It is quite obvious in the Genesis story why it is necessary for God to bless, because as the story goes, preceding the promise to Abraham, God has five times cursed.

> Cursed is the ground because of you;
> in toil you shall eat of it all the
> days of your life;

thorns and thistles it shall bring forth to you;

  ·   ·   ·   ·   ·   ·   ·   ·   ·   ·

you are dust,
    and to dust you shall return.

You are cursed from the ground, which has opened its mouth
to receive your brother's blood from your hand.

    Cursed be Canaan;
      a slave of slaves shall he be to his brothers.

In those curses and the rest of them, the Genesis stories cap-
ture all our misery—our enslavement of our fellowman, our
murderous warfare and injustice, our toil to overcome hunger
and poverty, the terrible futility of our death. If such distortions of life are the result of our flight from Yahweh, as
the Scriptures say they are, then we do indeed need a new
relationship with our God, in which his curse is turned into
blessing and our death is overcome by his life. And our text
says that it is by means of Abraham that God gives us life:
"I will bless those who bless you, Abraham, and him who
curses you I will curse."

All right then. Perhaps we should look more closely at that
ancient Semite and his people. Just who is this man called
Abraham, anyway? And how is it that we should consider
him blessed by the Lord?

In the first place, it is very clear from the Genesis stories
that Abraham is the man whose life is not his own. We hear
a lot of talk these days about "man come of age" and the
freedom of man to solve his own problems and to make his
own decisions and to chart his own destiny. But Abraham is
the man who has no such freedom. Every other Amorite of
the second millennium B.C. was free to migrate where he
would in search of better fortune, in a vast Semitic migration
that flooded the ancient Near East. But not Abraham. He
could not pick out his future home on the basis of his own
economic and personal considerations. He was given a specific
goal: the land that Yahweh would show him, a land neither
known to him nor chosen for its desirability. It was toward

that unknown land that Abraham had to direct his footsteps. And it was in that land that he had to live out all his days.

Was Abraham blessed by the Lord? He certainly wasn't ever free of him, because he found that any decision he made could never be a final decision. He had a troublesome maid named Hagar, of whom his wife was jealous. And so he allowed his nagging wife to send Hagar into the desert to die. "Your maid is in your power; do to her as you please," he decided—anything to have a little peace around the place. The difficulty was, that troublesome God sent Hagar back home again. And Abraham was forced to live with two bickering women in his tent.

Then there was the matter of a son to inherit his property. Abraham had never had an heir of his own. And so he chose the son of his slave, Eliezer of Damascus. He will be my son and heir, Abraham decided. But God said no: "In the spring of the year, Sarah your wife shall have a son." And Isaac was born, and Abraham's decision was overruled by the decision of the Lord. You see, Abraham had a very difficult time laying out his own future. Whenever he got his plans assembled, the Lord had different plans, and Abraham found himself constantly haunted by a will that was not his own.

He couldn't even be righteous and good all by himself. We think we can, of course. We think we can prove how compassionate and just we are by marching in a demonstration or by working for humanitarian causes or by making studies of the poor. But Abraham could be counted righteous only when he trusted Yahweh. The story tells of the night when God took him outside the tent. "Look toward heaven, and number the stars, if you are able to number them. . . . So shall your descendants be." Such was the promise of the Lord. And the passage continues, "And Abraham believed the Lord, and the Lord reckoned it to him as righteousness." Only when he trusted the promise of God was Abraham counted good. He had no goodness or worthiness apart from his Creator. In fact, when he tried to work out a moral way on his own, he ended up a liar, and he found himself in the humiliating situ-

175

ation of receiving a lecture on proper ethics from the heathen king of Egypt.

The patriarch of Israel just never controlled his own life. His actions, his decisions, his righteousness, always depended finally on Yahweh. He was a God-met man who could never break free of his constant divine companion. And whether we live or die depends on whether or not we think that kind of life is blessed.

Abraham is something else, however. He is not only a man whose life is not his own. He is also the man whose time is not yet. Last summer, one of the participants in our seminary's Lay School of Theology expressed dismay over the Bible's constant emphasis on the future. "If God is the Lord," he said, "why isn't his Lordship immediately evident? Why is everything postponed for the future? Why isn't the fulfillment of the Kingdom present here and now?" The questions were quite natural ones for our day and age. We are such an impatient people. We are always looking for immediate evidence, for immediate results, for immediate goals and victories. And the radical theologians among us throw out any statement they can't empirically prove at the moment.

But Abraham is the man who can never rely on the here and now. The meaning and the fulfillment of his life lie always in the future beyond him. The Genesis stories put it very clearly, in their own way. Abraham is promised the land for his own, but the Canaanites are still in the land. And Abraham is the man who has to wait until God fulfills his promise. His time is not yet; he has to walk in faith. And the only thing he has to go on is that promise, that word of Yahweh.

It is that way with Abraham's descendants all through the Old Testament. The psalmist finds himself weighed down with the burden of his sin, and out of the depths he cries to God and trusts in his coming forgiveness:

> I wait for the LORD, my soul waits,
> and in his word I hope;

176

        my soul waits for the LORD
            more than watchmen for the morning,
            more than watchmen for the morning.

A people forgotten and dead in exile are told that their plight
is not final, and that if they wait for God's redeeming act,
they shall renew their strength and soar up on wings like
eagles. A prophet cries out that justice is perverted and that
wicked men are prospering, drawing the innocent into their
nets of evil like fish caught in a sea. And again we have that
word which says there is a future planned by God:

            For still the vision awaits its time;
                it hastens to the end—it will not lie.
            If it seem slow, wait for it;
                it will surely come, it will not delay.

The time is not yet, you see. The Kingdom on earth is still
coming. We can't be satisfied with things as they are in our
present day. We can't rest content with any achievement or
consider any task to be done. Like Abraham, we have to consider it a blessed state to walk only by faith, and in hope.

Is that the blessed life? Is it good to believe without seeing, and to hope for a meaning beyond the present? Those
are the questions which are put to us by Abraham and his
people.

There is one more dimension to Abraham, according to our
text. Abraham is the man who must suffer for the purpose of
God. "Abraham, Abraham," the word of God comes one day,
"take your son, your only son Isaac, whom you love, and go
to the land of Moriah, and offer him there as a burnt offering upon one of the mountains of which I shall tell you." We
have a great deal of difficulty with such a story. We have
difficulty believing that God would command such a thing in
the first place. But we also have difficulty believing that a
grieving father, who knows that his only son must die, is in
any way the recipient of the goodness and blessing of God.

It has been my privilege throughout my life to know a num-

                        177

ber of suffering Christians. I remember such friends and relatives not primarily because they suffered. Heaven knows, all of us suffer at one time or another—if not sooner, then at some later date. But these people were distinguished by the fact that they suffered as Christians—that is, they were convinced that their pain or mental anguish or grievous circumstances could not separate them from the love of God they had known in Jesus Christ. And you know, a remarkable thing happened through those persons. Their faith in the midst of their anguish revealed God in a way impossible in normal circumstances. Those of us who watched their struggle saw a strength which simply was not humanly there, joy and humor displayed which could bear no relation to the pain undergone, peace conveyed in the midst of the most awful torment. It was as if such persons became totally transparent, so that through them shone, in undimmed splendor, the glory of the Lord. Moreover, something happened to those suffering Christians themselves. Those of us who knew them forgot all about their infirmities. Their cripplings were no longer seen, their problems no longer pitied. We simply stood in wondering admiration of the magnificence of their persons. I do not doubt that God uses the suffering of such persons for his own purposes, and that they are indeed, in a very unique way, blessed and favored by the Lord.

And I wonder if that is really not what Abraham and his people were all about—the suffering people on the face of the earth, through whose anguish the Lord made himself known. "You are my witnesses," Yahweh told the suffering Israel of Second Isaiah, and they were called to be the people who were wounded for our iniquities and bruised for our transgressions.

We don't want it that way, do we? We refuse to believe that a life of servanthood is the blessed life. And so we prattle endlessly about the freedom of man, and what we really mean is that we want to be our own gods. We see no particular good to be gained by walking only according to the promise, and so we rule out that kind of blessedness by explaining that a view of a God who promises and fulfills is now scientifically primitive. As for suffering for the purpose of God, everyone knows that is a barbarous view. God makes himself known, not in suffering, we say, but in harmonious interpersonal relationships. We just won't have it Abraham's way—mankind has never said yes to that Semite. And even in our present day, we try to be rid of the memory of him. We try to pretend that he never lived by trying to get rid of the Jews.

One of the more aggressive humanists in our community has a very telling attitude toward the Jews. She thinks it's just awful that some Jews refuse to marry with those outside their faith. It's that kind of exclusiveness, she complains, which is an offense to brotherhood. What we need is a community in which there are no such offensive people. Yes, let's get rid of the offensive Jews, if even under the guise of brotherhood—those awful people who bring with them the whisper of the memory of Abraham.

Even now, though Paul has said that disbelieving Jews have been rejected, the Jews trouble and disturb us Gentiles. For they are an obstacle to our self-rule. We have the uncomfortable feeling that perhaps we could be rejected too. They disturb us mysteriously with the thought that their rejection serves a greater purpose. And they make us uneasy because they are somehow a sign that the future is not in our hands.

So it is that we descend to our worst depths to get rid of the Jews, to wipe out those people who remind us of Israel, to be free of that Lord who haunted Israel's life. Come, let us get rid of the Jews, we cry, and we keep them out of our clubs and fraternities. We hound them from nation to nation. We shut them up in ghettos. We cremate them in the ovens of Nazism. And yes, we even pretend that we are the masters of the Jews, by issuing the Vatican decree that absolves them from their sin.

Perhaps that attempt to escape the Jews and the Lord who rules their lives is, in miniature, the same attempt we made that day in Jerusalem, when we hauled a man from Nazareth before Pontius Pilate for judgment. For who else was that man except the final Jew among us, the one who made it fully clear that we have to deal with God? Matthew puts it all in focus: Jesus Christ was the Son of God. But he was also the son of Abraham, Israel as Israel was meant to be, a whole people gathered into his one corporate person. He was the one man who fully knew that his life belonged to God. He was the one descendant of Abraham who knew how to walk in perfect trust. He was the only member of Israel who could become really that Suffering Servant, the only one who could bear our griefs and by whose stripes we are healed.

So it is that the decision we have to make about Abraham is finally a decision we have to make about Jesus Christ. As the final faithful son of Abraham, Jesus puts it squarely before us. If you want to have life and have it more abundantly, he tells us, then you must lose your life for my sake and for the Father's, because your life is not your own. You will live only if you walk by faith, only if you believe, even when you cannot see, that God is with you always and holds your decisions and destiny in his hands. You will live only as you learn to sacrifice yourself for God's purpose, only as you are willing to take up your cross and follow me. In Jesus of Nazareth, we see the fulfillment of Abraham in its full and final force, the chosen of God whose way of faith is the only way of blessing. The decision about the patriarch of Israel is finally a decision about Jesus Christ, because it is a choice to affirm or deny God's work in our world.

And what do we do when we confront that man who is the faithful Israel of God? We fall back on our ancient way out: "Crucify him!" we cry. "Let's get rid of that Jew!"

But you see, Jesus Christ is the descendant of Abraham of whom we cannot be rid, and confronting him, we have to come to some ultimate decision about that Jew and his God.

In his book about the trial of Adolf Eichmann, called *Justice in Jerusalem*, prosecuting attorney Gideon Hausner finds only one hope for a world that has known the horror of Auschwitz and Buchenwald—the people of Israel still live. Yes, the descendants of Abraham still live, but not only in the

180

manner and persons that Hausner imagines. Israel lives ultimately because Jesus Christ lives, because the son of Abraham is risen from the grave, because God has overcome our final attempt to get rid of his one faithful Jew. And that is the mercy of God, that he has not accepted our decision any more than he accepted Abraham's, that he has given us the chance once more to decide if we will be blessed or cursed.

Jesus Christ lives, and those of us who can bless his name and who can accept his way as blessed will enter into his life, as heirs of the promise to Abraham. That is not an easy way to choose. It means that we no longer own ourselves, that we cannot fulfill our own lives, that we give up ourselves to suffering if necessary for the purpose of God. But it is a decision we cannot avoid; it is a choice written into history: "I will bless those who bless you, and him who curses you I will curse." The final meaning of that promise has been made clear once for all. We choose the curse and death, or we choose life through Jesus Christ.

Amen.

C. USING A COMMON MOTIF

This sermon illustrates one of the ways the preacher can use motifs common to both Testaments to develop his presentation. I was invited by a group of women called The King's Daughters, in New Holland, Pennsylvania, to speak to them on the subject "Firm Foundations." No text was specified, and indeed the talk need not even have had the form of a sermon. However, the meeting was held in a church sanctuary and the sermon form seemed appropriate.

The sermon was developed through an examination of the various passages concerned with "foundations" in the two Testaments, and this approach immediately involved dealing with the motif of the "chaos" or "flood." The sermon illustrates how such Biblical language can be explained and translated for a modern congregation, while preserving the meaning of the original text. While the sermon deals with these motifs first of all as ideas, it should be noted that it is finally anchored in the salvation history, in the recounting of God's acts in creation and in the life, death, and resurrection of Jesus. Further, it is against the background of the salvation history that the ethical demands of the Lucan text are set. Without this background, such demands would have become mere moralisms without meaning.

FIRM FOUNDATIONS

Scripture Lessons: Psalm 104:1–9; Luke 6:46–49

I have been asked to say something this afternoon about the theme of your meeting, "Firm Foundations," and I must confess that this theme rather intrigues me, because, as you perhaps are aware, you are not the first group to think about this topic. The writers of our Bible, too, were very much concerned with the foundations of life—with those firm bases on which they could rest all their thoughts and actions. In fact, if you examine the Biblical passages dealing with foundations, you find that there were several fundamental things which the Biblical writers had to say, and it is these which I would like to discuss with you today.

First of all, the men of Biblical faith were quite sure that God intended that there be a basic God-given order in this life of ours. When he created the world, the Bible says, God created order, and this order reached down into the very foundations of the earth itself. The writer of Psalm 104 puts it this way:

> Thou didst set the earth on its foundations,
> so that it should never be shaken.

Now if we want to understand what that verse means, we must leave behind our twentieth-century ideas for a few minutes, and go back into that ancient world of 2000 B.C., which gave birth to the creation story in our Bible. In the beginning, Genesis says, the earth was *tohu wa-bohu,* that is, the earth was a watery chaos, a primeval deep, nothing but raging water and darkness over all the face of the globe. And God created this earth of ours by bringing order into the chaos. He said, "Let there be light," and so the chaotic darkness was conquered and given the bounds of the night. Darkness was rolled back and held in check by God's good gift of light. But still the raging waters covered the earth and there was no place for man to live. And so, according to the Genesis story, God created the firmament, the solid arc of the sky, which the ancients thought was like a solid piece of metal. And God lifted up the firmament to form the sphere of the sky, trapping some of the chaotic waters above the firmament and leaving some of them below. And then to the raging waters below, God said, "Let the dry land appear," and the waters of chaos were rolled back and held in bounds and the earth with its good land appeared—a flat earth, according to the ancient conception, floating on the waters. And then God gave foundations to the earth, anchoring it with pillars or mountains in the primeval ocean, so that despite the raging of the waters, it could not be moved.

> Thou didst set the earth on its foundations,
> so that it should never be shaken.

Such was the ancient view of the creation of the world.

This whole picture was more than simply a story of the creation to the men of the Bible, however. It was also symbolic of God's conquest of evil. The raging water, the primeval dark and chaotic deep, were symbols to the ancient mind of everything that was evil in this world, and when the men of the Bible said that God had put limits on the chaos, they meant that he had conquered evil. God controlled the forces of darkness and death and wrong; he held them in check; and because God ruled over the earth, order prevailed in men's lives —not only in the natural world around them but in their society and private lives as well. It was because God was the sovereign of his universe that man could live in peace and harmony. Thus the psalmist could sing his well-known song, using these symbols we have mentioned:

> God is our refuge and strength,
>> a very present help in trouble.
> Therefore we will not fear though the earth should change,
>> though the mountains shake in the heart of the sea;
> though its waters roar and foam,
>> though the mountains tremble with its tumult.

Evil, symbolized by the chaotic waters, could not threaten the psalmist, because God was his refuge and strength, a very present help in trouble. God created and intended that there be order in his world, and man could count on that order to be present as long as he trusted his God.

> Thou didst set the earth on its foundations,
>> so that it should never be shaken.

That was the statement of a psalmist who knew that God was in charge.

If there is one thing we do not have in this world of ours today, however, it is order, and indeed sometimes it seems as if we have returned to some primeval chaos. In our cities, muggings and murders keep us home behind locked doors at night, and we do indeed fear the darkness. In our homes, fathers lose touch with their sons, and parents are no longer honored. In our government, lies and injustices seem to abound, and we feel we can trust no politician. In our world, Arab and Jew continually teeter on the brink of an all-out war, Russian and Chinese troops mass against each other on the disputed border of their lands, Irish slaughter one another in the most senseless of civil wars. Chaos prevails between nation and nation, between black and white, old and young, rich and poor. And indeed, the very environment around us seems saturated with turmoil. Once we turned to the world of nature for rest and refreshment and peace. Now the air we breathe is polluted with deadly gases, our once-lovely rivers flow with filth and sewage and rotting waste, the trees fall before the highway crew or the newest suburban shopping center, birds on our coastlands die in the oil slicks left by tankers and oil drillers. Over the whole of our earth, it seems, chaos rules as king, and that chaos festers inside each of us in the form of fear and worry and unease. If we were to characterize the tenor of our times in a passage from the Bible, we would not choose the peaceful song of Psalm 104, but the apocalyptic picture of the prophet Isaiah:

> The foundations of the earth tremble.
> The earth is utterly broken,
>> the earth is rent asunder,
>> the earth is violently shaken.
> The earth staggers like a drunken man,
>> it sways like a hut;
> its transgression lies heavy upon it,
>> and it falls, and will not rise again.
>
> (Isa. 24:18–20.)

There are no firm foundations in our world today, it seems. Even our religion and morals are undergoing change. And we could easily adopt as our motto a line from Psalm 82: "All the foundations of the earth are shaken."

Moreover, we don't quite know what to do about the situation. It seems like much too easy an answer to say simply, "Trust in God," because most of us sitting in this church today already do trust in him. Occasionally you come across a billboard or a sign beside the highway that says, "Jesus is the answer," and, you know, somehow such a sign just doesn't quite ring true. Somehow it gives a much too simple answer to a much too complex problem. On one level, of course, the sign is true. Of course Jesus is the answer and the healing to this world's chaos. The question is, How do you and I apply that healing to our specific situation? Is it enough for us simply to believe, and does our belief make one bit of difference in bringing peace to the world or in curing the ills of our cities or in solving the problems of water and air pollution? Does the faith of you and me, as individuals, have any effect whatsoever on the turmoil of the world around us? No,

185

we have to admit that it usually does not, and we feel totally and utterly helpless, like the writer of another psalm who asked in sheer frustration, "If the foundations are destroyed, what can the righteous do?" (Ps. 11:3).

There is a final Biblical passage dealing with foundations which I would like to read to you. It comes from the sixth chapter of The Gospel According to Luke, and represents Luke's version of one of Jesus' teachings:

> Why do you call me "Lord, Lord," and not do what I tell you? Every one who comes to me and hears my words and does them, I will show you what he is like: he is like a man building a house, who dug deep, and laid the foundation upon rock; and when a flood arose, the stream broke against that house, and could not shake it, because it had been well built. But he who hears and does not do them is like a man who built a house on the ground without a foundation; against which the stream broke, and immediately it fell, and the ruin of that house was great. (Luke 6:46–49.)

In these words of our Lord, once again we have the picture of chaotic waters, symbolizing all the evil of life, rising up to threaten us, but this passage is first of all a comforting word to each of us. Jesus never glossed over the difficulties of living. He was not a dealer in "sweetness and light," as he is sometimes made out to be. How could he be when he knew that the torture of a cross lay before him? The flood will come, he said. The evil powers of darkness and turmoil, of wrong and pain and even death, will come. And they will beat against your life, and you will have to undergo them. "There's no hiding place down here." You too will be threatened by the primeval chaos.

But with me, Jesus said, you can withstand the waters. If you come to me and hear my words and carry them out, the evil flood will beat against your life and you will withstand it. Because, you see, God is the ruler over the chaos, after all. It was he who first set the light in the heavens and turned the darkness into a time of rest for man. It was he who established the stars in their orbits and first gave heat to the sun. It was

186

he who caused the plants to grow and filled the earth with color. It was he who set the earth on its foundations, so that it should never be shaken. But more than that, the God who created this earth of ours is also the God who sent his Son, who took all man's evil upon himself in the shape of a cross, who met all the worst that man could do and even underwent death, and yet who rose and conquered death and won out over all our wrong. Yes, God is still the ruler over our chaotic world, and with his Son we can withstand the onslaughts of the evil flood. "In the world," Jesus said, "you have tribulation; but be of good cheer, I have overcome the world."

Our Lord's words which we read from the passage in Luke are more than consolation, however. They are also a warning call to action to each of us who hears them. "Why do you call me 'Lord, Lord,' and not do what I tell you?" Jesus asks. "Every one who comes to me and hears my words and does them"—he is like the man who laid the foundation of his house upon rock. He is the one who has a firm foundation for his life. He is the one who can withstand the onslaughts of the flood. The person who hears Jesus' words and does them; the one who listens and obeys!

I suppose one of our greatest difficulties in understanding the teachings of Jesus is that we never feel they are directed specifically to us in our particular time and in our particular situation. We always seem to have the feeling that Jesus' words are meant to call us out of our situation into another field of endeavor. But nothing could be farther from the truth! Jesus speaks to each of us, as we are right now, and where we are in our everyday life. And it is there and to us that he says, "Why do you call me 'Lord, Lord,' and not do what I tell you?"

So the real answer to our chaotic times is to start doing what he tells us, isn't it? And that means to exercise his forgiveness in the situation where we are—in the misunderstanding which you have with your children, or in your quarrel with your husband, or in the dislike which you hold for another woman in this church. Yes, it means to exercise Christ's forgiveness even

187

toward those you don't understand—the bearded hippies, the rebellious young, the militant blacks, and the radical whites. What chaos could be avoided if only we could learn to forgive one another! Think of the hatred we could overcome in this county alone.

We must begin to do what Jesus tells us. And that means to imitate his care and concern for others. The Gospel tells us that a multitude followed Jesus to listen to his teaching, and that as the day wore on, the crowd had nothing to eat. And Jesus had compassion on them, because they were hungry, and he fed them with the miracle of loaves and fishes. Well, there are hungry people in this city also, and we must begin to feed them because we have Christ's compassion.

There were rejected souls in Jesus' time, just as there are in ours—the woman who was a sinner, a prostitute, the tax collectors who collaborated with the occupation forces—and Jesus ate with them at table and made them his friends. How our Lord was criticized for the company he kept! Who is rejected in the polite circles of your community these days—some divorced woman, or some poor man, or some black worker? We must begin to show them the care and concern Jesus had.

As for the issues of war and peace, how really dedicated are we to the Prince of Peace? We decorate the war hero with medals for bravery and put the conscientious objector in jail. Killing a man is a crime among us, until it's done on the battlefield. Then the youth who pulled the trigger becomes a candidate for the bronze star. How strange a way we go about trying to do the things Jesus tells us. "You have heard that it was said, 'An eye for an eye and a tooth for a tooth.' . . . But I say to you, Love your enemies. . . ."

In that psalm which says, "All the foundations of the earth are shaken," one reason is given for the chaos that reigns in man's society: those who could do something about it have failed to accept responsibility, and the afflicted are denied any justice, and the weak and the needy are ignored. And that is why, the psalmist says, the foundations of the earth are shaken. "Why do you call me 'Lord, Lord,' and not do what I tell you?"

Yes, despite all the chaos in our world, God is the ruler yet, and he can provide us with a firm foundation to withstand and overcome every evil. But there is a condition attached to our ability to find a secure basis for our lives, a condition that our victorious Lord makes very clear:

Every one who comes to me and hears my words and does them, I will show you what he is like: he is like a man building a house, who dug deep, and laid the foundation upon rock; and when a flood arose, the stream broke against that house, and could not shake it, because it had been well built.

Amen.

D. A COMBINATION OF METHODS

This sermon was preached to seminary students in the chapel of Lancaster Theological Seminary, Lancaster, Pennsylvania, and is thus perhaps a fitting conclusion to a book designed for clergymen. The sermon uses both of the methods of preaching from the Old Testament that we have discussed, that of promise and fulfillment, and that of analogy. First, an analogy is drawn between the function of the prophet in the Old Testament and that of the Christian preacher. Second, the word of God which the prophets proclaimed and acted out is finally seen to be incarnated in Jesus Christ, and as the final bearer of the word he becomes the model of all true prophets. It is finally his story and its meaning for us as his ministers which is proclaimed.

ON BEING A PROPHET [2]

Hymn: "God of the Prophets! Bless the Prophets' Sons"

Scripture Lessons: Ezekiel 13:1–16; John 1:14–18

"God of the prophets! bless the prophets' sons." This hymn, which we have just sung in our worship service, is very often used in the service of ordination to the Christian ministry. This is an indication of the fact that, in some sense, the ministry in the Christian church is understood as analogous to the ministry of the prophets of Israel.

Indeed, I suppose we might say that this is one of the highest goals which is set before us all—to have a prophetic ministry. There are few higher compliments which can be paid to a clergyman than to have someone say of him, "That man's a real prophet."

Undoubtedly a prophetic ministry is one that makes an impact on the church. By our modern definitions, a prophet in the pulpit is inevitably seen as a man of wisdom. He is a man who can discern God working in the events of our day. He is a man who knows the direction in which his world is heading. He is a man who can read "the signs of the times," and who can therefore influence the course of events sometimes before those events ever take place. Every Christian minister would like to be a man of such wisdom and influence. All of us would like to have a truly prophetic ministry.

In our desire to be prophets, we therefore should look again at just what a prophet is called to do. And this becomes quite clear in the passage from Ezekiel which we heard for our Scripture this morning. In this passage, God attacks the false prophets of Ezekiel's time. By the negative description Ezekiel gives us, the true role of a prophet is illumined.

In the first place and most obviously, God attacks the false prophets because they are prophesying out of their own minds. "They say, 'Says the Lord,' when the Lord has not sent them." In order to have something to preach about on the next festival day, the false prophets have been drawing on their own opinions, their own ideas, their own inspirations and reflections. And, of course, we all recognize ourselves and our fellows in such a description. Many of our sermons on Sunday morning are constructed of our own pet opinions. And too often our congregations are subjected to a Gospel strictly according to us. The true prophet is one who proclaims the word which

190

God has given him. It is a fact that we know, even if sometimes we do not put that knowledge into practice.

But the true prophet does more than this, according to Ezekiel. The true prophet refuses to mislead his people. He refuses to say to them "Peace," when there is no peace. Now of course that is a description with which we wholeheartedly agree! In our minds, a prophet is certainly one who preaches judgment.

I suppose the most common attitude to be found among new graduates of a seminary is an attitude of condemnation toward the church and its people. For three long and feverish years, you students have knowledge poured into you. Willingly or unwillingly, you all are forced to absorb at least something, and by the time you leave our doors, most of you are simply bursting to give something out. Indeed, if you are like I was when I left seminary, you wonder a bit how the church has survived so long without you. And so you can't wait to rush forth to tell your congregation where and why they are wrong.

We older seminary graduates must confess, however, that you are not alone in your pride. I think all of us—like Harry Truman—secretly love to "give 'em hell." It makes us feel so superior somehow, so wise, so all-knowing in our position. In fact, when we preach about judgment to the people, it makes us feel just like prophets. The people are wrong and sinful and stupid and weak, quite obviously, and all of us budding Isaiahs are determined to let them know it. Oh, yes, when it comes to pointing out people's faults, we have no lack of talent. And in our egotism, we foolishly think that this makes up the whole substance of the prophetic ministry.

But there is a third description of the false prophet in this passage from Ezekiel, and it is on this description that I would like to dwell this morning. Ezekiel says that his colleagues are false prophets for another reason: "You have not gone up into the breaches, or built up a wall for the house of Israel, that it might stand in battle in the day of the LORD." Ezekiel has drawn this description from military terminology. And he is

191

saying that the false prophets have failed to place themselves in the front ranks of the troops. They have not moved up to fill the gap in the line. They have not exposed themselves to maximum danger. They have not borne the brunt of the enemy's attack in Israel's day of battle.

You see, according to this passage from Ezekiel, whether we know it or not, you and I and our churches and congregations are engaged in warfare. We are fighting a life-and-death battle in which we will win or lose all. We are being attacked by an enemy who can snuff out our lives for all eternity. And that enemy is not Russia or China with their atomic bombs, for they really have no power in the final reckoning. The enemy is not Satan or death, for they have already lost the battle. No, it is very clear from the words of Ezekiel that our enemy is God. He it is who is attacking you and me and the people we represent. God is the one who can do us forever to death. "Do not fear those who kill the body but cannot kill the soul; rather fear him who can destroy both soul and body in hell"— God, the ruler over heaven and hell. God is the one against whom we have to wage the battle. And it is the Day of the Lord that brings the life-and-death struggle to its climax.

That is shocking for us who have been raised on comfort and security from our religion: to think that God is in any way an enemy to us. Our God is not a God who battles us; our God is a God of love, we say. And so we have no idea what it really means to say we must have peace with God. And we don't really believe that our sin has created a no-man's-land between ourselves and our Maker.

But the truth is there—in all the long history of Israel it is there: God, the outraged husband charging his people, his wife, with harlotry; God the Father declaring, "Sons have I reared and brought up, but they have rebelled against me." God the Creator crying out, "Be appalled, O heavens, at this, be shocked, be utterly desolate, . . . my people have committed two evils: they have forsaken me."

We blandly reply, Ah, but that was the old Israel, not the

new. And then we go about our business, unaware of our sinful rebellion. We get very angry at other people for the wrong they do. We rightly shake our heads and mutter ominous thoughts about those who deny minorities their civil rights and refuse to change our racist society. But we seldom stop to think that our long years of apathy have made us accessories to the crime. And we forget that we therefore nailed another darkskinned innocent man to a cross one day, and then we covered over his dead body in a borrowed grave and cursed him as an agitator.

We hate the ultraconservative for his blind attempt to write his own laws for society. But we take God's laws and alter them to suit our prides and whims. After all, "the New Testament ethic is an impossible demand."

We launch a global assault on communism and try to block its path in Vietnam and the Middle East. But all the time we too are materialistic atheists, looking for the church job that offers the nicest parsonage.

Let's be consistent when we start applying our labels to the human race. Let's get ourselves labeled a little more accurately in the Kingdom of God. You and I, along with the rest of them, are the subversives, the extremists, the red-necks in that Kingdom. And because of it, we have made ourselves and our people enemies of our God and King. Our sin and the sin of our congregations have turned our Ruler against us. That is the message of this passage in Ezekiel. And so God is attacking us to put down our revolt. Because we have rebelled against him, he is the enemy with whom we must contend.

If we look further at this passage in Ezekiel, it also becomes very clear that one person is called upon to bear the major force of God's attack. One man is asked to bear the primary onslaught of the enemy. And that man is the prophet, who must go up into the breach. That one is the man in the pulpit, if you will.

We tend to think sometimes that the prophets of the Old Testament get off more easily than those people upon whom they are called to pronounce judgment—as if somehow the fact that they are preachers exempts them from military duty. But if you look at the writings of the prophets, it is clear that they themselves suffer first in Israel.

God is going to discipline his whoring bride of a people. And so Hosea, too, must first find himself married to a harlot. And he sits and watches his children at play and knows that they are not really his. God is abandoning his house and heritage, and so Jeremiah must leave his home too. And the men of his native Anathoth become those who seek his life. God is giving the beloved of his eyes, the temple on Zion, to destruction. And so Ezekiel too must give up his loved wife to the oblivion of the grave.

The prophets of Israel do not escape the attack of God the enemy. They experience in their own lives the first wave of that attack, until, for Jeremiah, the Lord becomes a dread warrior with him and he must cry out in torment at the sounds he hears in his ears:

> My anguish, my anguish! [he moans] I writhe in pain!
> Oh, the walls of my heart!
> My heart is beating wildly;
> I cannot keep silent;
> for I hear the sound of the trumpet,
> the alarm of war.

Ezekiel is one of those chosen to announce the siege and destruction of Jerusalem. But it becomes the prophet first who must eat the meager rations of siege, cooked over unclean dung. And it is Ezekiel first of all who experiences the captivity of the exile, sent into a rigid stupor in which he cannot move from side to side.

It is the function of the prophets in the Bible to suffer first on behalf of their doomed people. And the modern prophet in the pulpit is called to no lesser fate. You may preach God's judgment upon your sinful congregations. Indeed, at times you must preach God's judgment. But if you would be a prophet, you should expect to experience that judgment before anyone else in your own life. God will subject your sinful people to pain, to loss, to worry and grief and despair. But as their prophet, you are bound up in the bundle of life with them. And you are asked to endure with them and for them these results of God's attack against sin. Do not look for a peaceful, trouble-free ministry if you would be a prophet. Look for the war wounds and weeping and suffering for sin of a Jeremiah or of an Ezekiel.

These prophets of the Old Testament fight back against the enemy. They refuse to allow the battle line to give way. They refuse to give up their sinful folk without a last-ditch effort. And everywhere we hear them pleading and praying with the Lord to spare their sinful people. There is Moses on Sinai forty days and nights, begging God to overlook that golden calf. There is Amos—the prophet of justice, we call him—in intercession for Israel:

> O Lord GOD, forgive, I beseech thee!
> How can Jacob stand?
> He is so small!

And finally there is Paul of Tarsus, wishing himself accursed and cut off from Christ for the sake of his brother Israelites.

Everywhere the prophet in the Bible is an intercessor for his sinful people, so much so that God must finally tell Jeremiah to stop bothering him with all those prayers: "As for you, do not pray for this people, or lift up cry or prayer for them, and do not intercede with me, for I do not hear you." If we would have a prophetic ministry, we must be as stubborn as Jeremiah, refusing to deliver one soul over to destroying judgment, refusing to give up hope for the saddest, most ignorant sinner among our acquaintances.

That's easy to do with the people we like. But how about the people we dislike? How about that man you have in your church who will not contribute a penny and who criticizes you to everyone he knows? How about that woman in the circle who is so self-righteous that she makes you sick with anger? And yes, how about that racial bigot or that leftist or that

Birchite whom you even now despise? Can you refuse to give these souls up too? Will you go up into the breach in their defenses, and stand there and turn aside, time after time, the onslaught of God against these people? Will you pray for them and intercede for them and love them and try time and time again to convey the full meaning of the gospel to them, so that they may stand in battle in the Day of the Lord? That's the task expected of you if you would be a prophet.

For, you see, the thing that makes a man a prophet is that he bears the word of God. And to be a prophet you've got to act in accordance with that word. But what does the word do? What were his actions when the Word of God made flesh walked this earth in our midst? He refused to give up one soul among us, too. He saw the gaping hole in our lines, up there on the front of the battle. He saw that we were doomed to destruction unless he placed his own body in that breach. He saw that we subversives and red-necks and extremists in the Kingdom of God could not possibly stand in battle when God attacked. And so he gave himself that we might go unharmed in the Day of the Lord. And his death on the fringe of no-man's-land kept us alive before the enemy.

Indeed, here is the wonder of the story: that Jesus Christ was not only a man on our side in the battle. He was an envoy sent by the enemy himself. He was sent over the line by the King of our country to take our side in the fray. And our enemy, the King, himself provided the means for our salvation and for our peace.

So it is that God too never gave up on us. He too refused to surrender one soul to eternal damnation. He would rather his own Son died than relinquish one rebel among us. No matter what the cost, he was determined to save the people in his realm.

It is finally the love of God, then, that makes a man a prophet. It is being possessed by the envoy of love, Jesus Christ, the Word of God incarnate. It is proclaiming and acting out the full sacrifice and mercy of that Word.

You are not a prophet merely because you are wise and can

discern the signs of the times. You are not a new Ezekiel simply because you pronounce judgment on your people. You are a prophet sent by God only when you also go up into the breach, and build up a wall for the house of the new Israel, that it may stand through Jesus Christ in battle in the Day of the Lord.

Amen.

Notes

Chapter I. THE LOSS OF THE BIBLE IN THE CHURCH

1. James D. Smart, *The Strange Silence of the Bible in the Church: A Study in Hermeneutics* (The Westminster Press, 1970).

2. See Brevard S. Childs, *Biblical Theology in Crisis* (The Westminster Press, 1970).

3. Scholarly debate still continues on this issue, e.g., in the writings of Wolfhart Pannenberg and F. Flückiger, to name only two.

4. Childs, *op. cit.*, pp. 54 ff.

5. John Bright, *The Authority of the Old Testament* (Abingdon Press, 1967).

Chapter II. HOW THE OLD TESTAMENT WAS LOST

1. The material in this chapter is absolutely necessary to our discussion, but makes no claim to be either original or exhaustive. I am principally indebted to Herbert F. Hahn, *The Old Testament in Modern Research* (Fortress Press, 1966, expanded ed.); Robert C. Dentan, *Preface to Old Testament Theology* (Yale University Press, 1950); Bright, *op. cit.*

2. S. J. De Vries, "Biblical Criticism, History of," *The Interpreter's Dictionary of the Bible* (Abingdon Press, 1962), Vol. I, p. 414a.

3. Dentan, *op. cit.*, p. 8.

4. W. A. Teller, *Topice Sacrae Scripturae* (1761).

5. W. F. Hufnagel, *Handbuch der Biblischen Theologie* (1785–1789).

6. *Ibid.*, pp. xiv–xv.

7. Dentan, *op. cit.*, p. 7.

8. Robert Lowth, *Praelectiones Academicae de Sacra Poesi Hebraeorum* (Oxford).

9. Dentan, *op. cit.*, p. 12.

10. Hahn, *op. cit.*, p. 7.

11. *Ibid.*, pp. 46–47.

12. See *ibid.*, pp. 63–68.

13. Émile Durkheim, *Les Formes Élémentaires de la Vie Religieuse* (Paris, 1912).

14. De Vries, *op. cit.*, p. 415ab.

15. Bright, *op. cit.*, pp. 102–103.

16. I have given this name to popular American religion simply because so much of it is propagated by slick-cover periodicals such as *The Reader's Digest,* and because that magazine is so typical in its sustenance of the phenomenon. But *The Reader's Digest* is by no means solely responsible for or the only representative of our popular religion.

Chapter III. THE RESULTS OF THE LOSS OF THE OLD TESTAMENT: THE LOSS OF THE NEW TESTAMENT AND THE DEVELOPMENT OF " 'READER'S DIGEST' RELIGION"

1. Not only does the Old Testament understand the processes of nature (Gen. 8:22; Ps. 65:9 ff.; 135:7; 147:8–9, 15–18) and the earth's ecology (Ps. 104) to be effects of the wise and faithful working of God, but it also understands the structure of the universe and the preservation of cosmic order over against chaos as the result of God's active sustenance of his creation (Gen. 9:8 ff.; Ps. 89:9; Neh. 9:6; cf. Jer. 4:23–26).

2. Throughout the Old Testament, the natural world therefore is used by God to serve his purpose, whether of judgment or of salvation. Disasters in nature can be his instruments of judgment (Ex., chs. 7 to 12; Ps. 105:28 ff.; Amos 4:7–9; I Kings 17:1), as nature's bounty can be the gift of his grace (Deut. 28:1–14; Ps. 105:41–42), and it is taken for granted that all creation praises its Creator (Ps. 148).

3. The Old Testament therefore never hesitates to speak of

the transformation of this world (Isa. 11:6–9; 40:4; 54:10; 65:17) or of its disappearance altogether (Isa. 51:6; Ps. 102:25–26).

4. The Priestly tradition in Gen., chs. 1 to 2:4a emphasizes God's otherness from his creation by making the divine Word the sole contact of God with his world (cf. John 1:3), and by removing the creation from the mythical world of timelessness and placing it firmly within the scheme of history (Gen. 2:4a).

5. "Prayer for Today," by J. R. Brokhoff, *Lancaster Intelligencer Journal* (Lancaster, Pa.: Steinman and Steinman, Inc.).

6. It was therefore not surprising that John A. T. Robinson's suggestion that we see God in, with, and under everything that exists met with instant acceptance. (*Honest to God* [The Westminster Press, 1963].)

7. This is emphasized in the blessing in Gen. 1:28 and in J's view that man lives only when his body is animated by the breath of God (Gen. 2:7).

8. In Gen. 2:4b to 11:9, the Yahwist sets the history of all mankind in the framework of this decision, whereas the other great histories of the Old Testament (P, D, the Chronicler) concentrate their attention specifically upon Israel's faithfulness or unfaithfulness. But the prophets too pronounce God's judgment on all the nations in terms of this turning.

9. Even the legalistic ethical systems that are often found in the church are a manifestation of humanism, in that they are based on a human calculation of what man deserves rather than on a witness to what God has done for him.

10. The ethic of Deuteronomy, which was to be definitive for Israel (Deut. 4:2), rested upon the central presupposition that God had acted in love toward Israel (Deut. 7:6–8) and that Israel's obedience to his commandments was her loving response to his love (Deut. 6:4–5), which issued in mercy toward others (cf. Deut. 24:17–22). In Hosea, God's knowledge of Israel was to issue in her knowledge and faithfulness toward him in her actions in the world (Hos. 13:4–6). Throughout the New Testament, it is God's act in Jesus Christ which is to furnish the model for the church's action in the world (Eph. 5:1–2; I John 4:7 ff.; Matt. 5:48; John 13:34–35; etc.).

11. One of the criteria for the prophets' definition of false

gods is the fact that they cannot do anything, that they do not have the power to bring about events. Cf. I Kings, ch. 18; Jer. 10:1–10; Isa., ch. 46; and throughout Deutero-Isaiah.

12. Thus, Israel's creedal statements (Deut. 26:5–9; 6:21–23; Josh. 24:2–13), her cultic hymns, laments, and thanksgivings (cf. The Psalms), her prophetic torah (Jer. 2:2–3; 2:4–13; Hos. 11:1–4; Amos 2:9–11; etc.), and her theology all take the form of confessing what Yahweh has done.

13. Cf. the central commandment of Deut. 6:4–5, as well as the prophets' constant calls for trust (Isaiah), for intimate knowledge of God (Hosea and Jeremiah), for love (Hosea), for faithfulness (Hosea, Jeremiah, Isaiah, Ezekiel) on the part of Israel toward her divine Husband and Father.

14. Isa. 29:13–14; 1:10–17; Jer. 7:1–26; Hos. 5:15 to 6:6; Amos 5:21–24.

15. God is therefore Israel's Father, and Israel is his son (Ex. 4:22; Deut. 8:5; 32:18; Isa. 1:2; 63:8, 16; Jer. 3:19; Hos. 11:1; Mal. 1:6).

16. Even Deuteronomy, which emphasizes that God's actions toward Israel are acts done out of love, nevertheless places that love in the framework of the divine purpose of bringing blessing on all mankind (Deut. 7:6–8).

17. Such is the import of the call to Abraham in Gen. 12:1–3, which is deliberately placed by the Yahwist against the background of the story of all men's sin and God's curse upon them, in Gen., chs. 2 to 11.

18. It is clear that some portions of the Old Testament not only envision Israel as the instrument through which God will restore his fellowship with mankind (Isa. 19:23–25; Zech. 8:20–23; 14:9, 16 ff.; Zeph. 3:9; Isa. 2:2–4), but also envision a time when the national boundaries of the people of God will be transcended to include all nations in the covenant fellowship of Israel (Ps. 47; Isa. 44:3c–5).

Chapter IV. THE NATURE OF THE OLD TESTAMENT

1. I have long been indebted to my former teacher, Gerhard von Rad, and his brilliant *Old Testament Theology* (English ed., London: Oliver & Boyd, Ltd., Vol. I, 1962, Vol. II, 1965) for my general approach to, and organization of, the

material in the Old Testament. However, while accepting von Rad's schema, I have dealt with the contents of the Old Testament in my own way and must be held solely responsible for the formulations of this chapter.

2. A *Heilsgeschichte* is a history which is initiated by the word of God, and then runs its course according to the working of that word, until the word is fulfilled.

3. It seems impossible to divide the material on the basis of a Tetrateuch-Deuteronomic History, as many scholars do, because of the prominent place which the promise to the patriarchs holds in Deuteronomy, not only in its ancient creeds (Deut. 26:5–9; 6:20–24), but also in its hortatory presentations of Yahweh's saving deeds (Deut. 1:8, 35; 4:1, 31, 37; 6:3, 10, 18, 23; 7:6, 8, 13; 8:1, 18; 9:5; 10:11; 11:9; etc.). The same emphasis continues in Joshua (Josh. 1:6; 5:6; 18:3; 21:43–44), so that the creedal summary of the Hexateuchal tradition history at the founding of the tribal confederation in Josh., ch. 24, only sums up that which has gone before. It would seem to ignore the principal thrusts of the text were we to divide such a history in two.

4. Von Rad clearly shows how this is so in his last book, *Weisheit in Israel* (Neukirchen-Vluyn: Neukirchener Verlag, 1970).

5. The one exception is the use of the tradition in the royal Psalm 72 (v. 17). There the promise of blessing on all nations is mediated through the anointed Davidic king, a fact that is of interest for the New Testament's interpretation.

6. Cf. the forceful presentations of the two traditions of Saul's rejection in I Sam., chs. 13 and 15, in which it is made very clear that it is Saul's failure over against the word of God which leads to his downfall (especially I Sam. 13:13–14; 15:23–26).

7. The use of the term for "covenant love" (*chesed*, consistently translated "steadfast love" in the RSV) leads the interpreter to expect that there would be mention of an eternal covenant between Yahweh and the Davidic house, in II Sam., ch. 7. Apparently this part of the original tradition has fallen out of the Samuel passage, but that there was indeed a covenant with David is affirmed by the older tradition of II Sam.

23:5, which is then echoed in the royal Psalms 132 and 89 (Ps. 132:11–12 and Ps. 89:3–4).

8. Note the constant emphasis in Deuteronomy and the D History on obedience and faithfulness to God as a matter of the heart. There is no legalism here, but the realization that he who truly loves God also obeys his commandments. And the love which is called for is consistently said to be motivated by Yahweh's loving deeds of salvation toward Israel. Israel was to love, because God first loved her. Cf. Deut. 7:6, 11, *et passim.*

9. Martin Noth, *Überlieferungsgeschichtliche Studien,* zweite unveränderte Auflage (Tübingen: Max Niemeyer Verlag, 1957), p. 5.

10. Specifically, Saul's disobedience consists in violation of the rules of the ancient holy war, which was a sacral institution of the tribal confederacy in the time of the Judges and whose ideology has been incorporated into Deuteronomy. Cf. Gerhard von Rad, *Der heilige Krieg im alten Israel* (Zurich: Zwingli Verlag, 1951); *Studies in Deuteronomy* (London: SCM Press, Ltd., 1948). According to those sacral rules, Israel's wars against her enemies were Yahweh's wars, to be carried out according to strict cultic regulations. They were to be preceded by vows, ceremonial cleansing of the camp, dedication of weapons, priestly sacrifice and inquiring of Yahweh. It is this latter requirement which Saul violates in I Sam., ch. 13, and which is presupposed in Deut. 20:2–4, although Deuteronomy's centralization of the cult has suppressed the account of the sacrifice. Following the battle, in which Yahweh terrified the enemy and won the victory, captives and booty were then to be dedicated to Yahweh in the ancient rite of *cherem,* and it is this requirement which Saul violates in I Sam., ch. 15. This law remains intact in Deuteronomy's appropriation of the holy war ideology (Deut. 7:16–26; 20:10–18), and I Sam. 15:1–3 refers specifically to Deut. 25:17–19.

11. So too I Kings 9:4; 11:4, 33; 15:3, 5; II Kings 22:2; *et al.*

12. Only in I Kings 15:5 is there a brief mention of David's murder of Uriah. Otherwise David's sin goes unnoticed in D.

13. This view is summarized in Solomon's blessing of the people at the time of the dedication of the Temple (I Kings 8:14–21; cf. ch 11:13, 32, 36). The importance of the dwelling

of Yahweh's name in the Temple is then emphasized in the prayer that follows (I Kings 8: 29, 33, 44, 48, etc.).

14. This is consistently expressed by the Deuteronomic phrase that the Lord "gives rest" to his people Israel, from all their enemies round about.

15. Cf., e.g., II Kings 16:2–4.

16. Only two kings after Solomon escape this judgment—Hezekiah (II Kings, ch. 18) and Josiah (II Kings, chs. 22 and 23), both of whom undertook wide-ranging reforms of Judah's religious life. However, the good acts of these two reformers are insufficient to overcome the judgment due Judah because of Manasseh's sins (II Kings 21:10 ff.; 23:26; 24:3).

17. The working of the word to David is consistently one of grace in the D History, in that it continually serves to postpone Judah's deserved destruction (I Kings 11:36; 15:4; II Kings 8:19).

18. The Levites are made the true bearers of the Ark (I Chron. 15:2–15), the keepers of the holy objects in the Temple (I Chron. 23:28–32), the teachers of the Torah under Jehoshaphat (II Chron. 17:7–9), and even scribes (I Chron. 24:6; II Chron. 34:13) and prophets (II Chron. 20:14–17). In II Chron. 29:34, it is stated, "The Levites were more upright in heart than the priests in sanctifying themselves."

19. E.g., although I Chron. 20:1 borrows the Succession Narrative's language from the beginning of the story of David's sin with Bathsheba (II Sam. 11:1), that entire story is omitted, as are all the vivid pictures of David's faults.

20. The term *bachar*, in the sense of "to choose, elect," is used sixteen times in the Chronicler's history, but its object is always the king (I Chron. 28:4; 29:1), the cult place of Jerusalem (II Chron. 7:12, 16; 12:13; 33:7), or the tribe of Levi (I Chron. 15:2; II Chron. 29:11). The only exception (I Chron. 16:13) is a quotation from Ps. 105.

21. Ps. 2; 18; 20; 21; 45; 72; 89; 101; 110; 132. Of these, probably only Ps. 45 comes to us from the Northern Kingdom.

22. Ps. 2:7–9; 110:1, 4; 132:11–12; cf. the prophetic theophany of Ps. 18:7–15.

23. The Hebrew has "I will be" in place of "where." This reading is adopted by James Merrill Ward, *Hosea: A Theological Commentary* (Harper & Row, Publishers, Inc., 1966),

pp. 20 ff., and may be correct. If so, it would emphasize Yahweh's personal destruction of his people.

24. Cf. the communal prayers and Yahweh's attitude toward them preserved for us in Hos. 5:15 to 6:6; Jer. 14:1–10. Cf. also the complacent confidence of the people, mirrored in Hos. 8:2; Jer. 5:12–13; Zeph. 1:12; Amos 5:14; 6:1–3; 9:10; Micah 2:6. Much confidence was placed in the Temple and Yahweh's presence on Zion (Jer. 7:4; 8:19; Micah 3:11), in the Davidic monarchy (Jer. 21:13), in the possession of the covenant (Jer. 8:8), in the promise of the land (Ezek. 33:23–24), and even in the failure of the prophetic word of judgment to produce immediate results (Ezek. 12:21–28; Isa. 28:9–10; cf. Jer. 18:18).

25. Deuteronomy's admonition to obedience and confidence in the future is based upon a recounting of Yahweh's works of love toward Israel in the past saving history.

26. The reader can imagine the effect of this announcement on Israel if he envisions a modern-day prophet proclaiming that the New Testament events no longer have any power to save the church from the destruction which God will bring upon it in his wrath. Our reaction would surely be the same as Israel's —disbelief, scorn and hatred of the prophet, finally hopelessness and despair.

27. Amos 9:11–15 are usually denied to that prophet, but Amos is from the South and these may very well be his words.

28. The reader should note that the judgment of Yahweh is pictured by the postexilic prophets as an event that still lies in the future, so that there is not a complete identification of the exile with the Final Judgment of Yahweh. To be sure, the exile is part of that judgment, but not its total fulfillment. This is important to remember in interpreting Second Isaiah, whose total message—including the death of the Servant—concerns the future.

29. This is especially emphasized in Ezekiel, where the destruction of Israel serves to teach the people: "Then they shall know that I am the LORD."

30. This holds true also of the nations' attitude toward Israel. The judgment of Israel serves only to convince them that Israel has been rejected by her God (cf. Isa. 53:2–3, 4cd).

31. This is very clear in Hos., ch. 14, where the prophet en-

visions Israel's repentance (Hos. 14: 2–3), and yet rests the salvation of Israel on Yahweh's healing and love (Hos. 14:4).

32. I am, of course, aware of the difficulties in determining the identity of the Servant of the Lord in Second Isaiah. My position is that the Servant Songs are an integral part of Second Isaiah and that the Servant is the sinful Israel of the past, who is to be transformed by the Spirit of Yahweh into his witness to the nations in the future.

33. Jer. 31:34; Isa. 40:2; 43:25; 44:22; 55:7; Zech. 3:9.

34. Isa. 35:9–10; 41:14; 43:1, 14; 44:6, etc.; 60:16; 62:12; Zech. 10:8.

35. Isa. 35:4; 43:3, 11; 45:21 f.; etc.

36. Isa. 10:24–27; 11:16; 48:20; 51:9–11; 52:11–12; 55:12; Jer. 23:7–8; cf. Isa. 52:3–6; 58:8; Zech. 2:7; 10:11.

37. Hos. 2:14–15; Isa. 41:17–20; 43:19–21; 48:21; 49:9–11.

38. Jer. 31:31–34; 32:40; Isa. 61:8. The covenant formula ("They shall be my people and I shall be their God"), or part of it, appears in all the following passages and signifies Yahweh's reestablishment of his covenant relationship with his people: Hos. 2:23; Jer. 24:7; 32:38; Ezek. 34:24, 30–31; 36:28; 37:23, 27; Isa. 51:16; Zech. 8:8.

39. Isa. 49:19–21; 54:1–3; 60:22; Jer. 23:3; Ezek. 36:37–38; Zech. 10:8–10.

40. Hos. 11:10–11; Zeph. 3:20; Jer. 24:4–6; 29:10; 31:7–9; 32:37; Ezek. 20:42; 34:13; 36:8; 37:12, 14; Zech. 10:8–10.

41. Nahum 1:15; Jer. 31:6, 14; Ezek. 20:40; Mal. 3:3–4; Jer. 33:18, 21; Isa. 27:12–13. Jer. 3:16 forbids the restoration of the Ark, however.

42. Jeremiah, Ezekiel, and Second Isaiah all affirm in the strongest terms the promise to the fathers. In Jeremiah and Ezekiel, the emphasis is on the promise of the land (cf. Jer. 3:18; 7:7, 14; 11:5; 16:15; 24:10; etc.; Ezek. 20:42; 36:28; 37:25; 47:14), in Second Isaiah, on the promise of descendants (Isa. 51:2; cf. ch. 41:8). Cf. also Micah 7:20. Second Isaiah even recalls God's promise to Noah (Isa. 54:9).

43. Amos 9:11; Isa. 11:1; 32:1; Micah 5:2; Jer. 23:5; Ezek. 34:23–24; 37:24–25; Hag. 2:23; Zech. 3:8; 9:9.

44. Uniquely in Zech. 6:13, the Davidic ruler is to share his rule with the high priest, in a dyarchy.

45. Jeremiah especially formulates the new Israel's future as a return to normalcy (Jer. 30:18–20; 31:4–6; 32:15, 43–44; 33:7, 10–11, 13; but cf. also Amos 9:14–15; Zech. 8:4–5).

46. Ezek. 36:35 and Isa. 51:3 call it "Eden."

47. Zeph. 3:15; Zech. 2:10–11; Joel 2:27; cf. Hag. 1:13; 2:4.

48. Ezek. 43:1–5; Isa. 40:9–11; 52:7–8; Zech. 1:17; 2:12; 3:2; cf. Isa. 24:23; 33:17–22. Haggai and Zechariah hold that the rebuilding of the Temple is the precondition of Yahweh's return to Zion and the beginning of the new age, since the people's attitude toward Yahweh is mirrored in their attitude toward the Temple reconstruction (Hag. 2:15–19; Zech. 8:9 ff.).

49. As von Rad has pointed out, there existed from pre-exilic times the tradition of the invincibility of Jerusalem before the onslaught of the nations (cf. the Psalms of Zion, 46; 48; 76), a tradition passed on most prominently in the oracles of Isaiah (Isa. 17:12–14; 10:27b–34; 14:28–32; 29:1–8; 30:27–33; 31:1–9), but also in Micah 4:11–13; Ezek., chs. 38 and 39; Joel 3:9–17. Thus the traditions concerning Zion in the new age revive ancient expectations which were proclaimed by Isaiah but never fulfilled.

50. This total reliance on Yahweh is pictured not only in terms of the new people's humble and contrite trust in Yahweh alone (Isa. 57:15; 66:2; cf. Zeph. 3:12), but also by saying that the new people are the blind and deaf and dumb, the lame and afflicted and imprisoned, to whom Yahweh has given the power to see, to hear, to speak, to walk, to come forth into the light (Isa. 61:1–3; 35:5–6; 42:16; cf. Jer. 31:8; Ezek. 34:16; Isa. 42:19–20; 43:8).

51. Isa. 19:24–25; 44:3; 61:9; Jer. 4:2; Zech. 8:13; Mal. 3:12, all look forward to the fulfillment of this part of the promise to Abraham.

Chapter V. The Relation of the Two Testaments

1. It is for this reason that von Rad's theological methodology is to be preferred over that of Walther Eichrodt, of John Bright in his *The Authority of the Old Testament,* and of G. Ernest Wright in his most recent writings. All would extract from the Old Testament a "structure of faith," typical of Israel's

theology at every period. But it is difficult to reduce Israel's constantly shifting interaction with the word of God to a static structure, brilliant and helpful as the attempts of these three scholars to do so have been.

2. E.g., the testing of Abraham in Gen., ch. 22, which was originally a cult saga legitimating the redemption of a child from sacrifice, has taken on a vastly deeper and more important meaning by being placed in the context of the promise of descendants to Abraham. Now the concern is with God's presence in history.

3. Walther Eichrodt, *Theology of the Old Testament,* Vol. I, tr. by J. A. Baker, The Old Testament Library (The Westminster Press, 1961).

4. I am indebted to my husband, Dr. Paul J. Achtemeier, professor of New Testament at Union Theological Seminary, Richmond, Va., for his invaluable criticisms and suggestions concerning my presentation of the New Testament material, although he cannot be held responsible for the use to which I have put them. In addition, I have used Reginald H. Fuller, *The Foundations of New Testament Christology* (Charles Scribner's Sons, 1965), as a control on my interpretation of the New Testament evidence.

5. Just the fact that we have four different Gospels testifies to this continual process of reshaping the traditions.

6. The Synoptic Gospels ultimately derive the figure of the Son of Man from pre-Christian Jewish apocalyptic tradition, as that is represented in Dan., ch. 7, the books of Enoch and IV Ezra. There is evidence in Mark 8:38 and Luke 12:8 that Jesus shared the Jewish belief in the coming transcendent Son of Man.

7. Fuller, *op. cit.,* p. 131.

8. *Ibid.*

9. It is worth noting that a partial synthesis of the Son of Man with royal ideology occurs already in I Enoch, where the Son of Man is called "His Anointed" (I Enoch 48:10; 52:4) and enjoys dominion on the throne of glory (I Enoch, chs. 45 to 69).

10. So Fuller, *op. cit.,* p. 157.

11. Acts 11:20 and ch. 16:31 portray the early preaching to the Gentiles as the proclamation of the Lordship of Jesus, in

whom converts then confessed their faith and were baptized.

12. It is difficult to see why this pericope would have been introduced by Mark and especially preserved in Matthew and Luke if it is not genuine reminiscence, since it contradicts the tradition of the Davidic descent of the Messiah.

13. The term "Messiah" comes from the Hebrew *mashiach,* "anointed," since Israel's kings were anointed to office, as a symbol of the gift of the Spirit which would enable them to rule. Priests too were anointed, but this is not found before P. "Christ," *christos,* is the Greek translation of the term.

14. Fuller, *op. cit.,* pp. 158–159.

15. Luke attempts to smooth over this contradiction in his note in Luke 3:23; "the son (as was supposed) of Joseph."

16. So Fuller, *op. cit.,* p. 24.

17. Contra those New Testament scholars who have maintained that the New Testament's use of the title is derived solely from the Hellenistic divine-man concept.

18. So Fuller, *op. cit.,* pp. 68–72, 192–197.

19. *Ibid.,* pp. 195–196.

20. Gen. 49:24; Ps. 23:1; 80:1; Isa. 40:11; Jer. 31:10; Ezek. 34:15.

21. Num. 27:17; I Kings 22:17; Isa. 44:28; 56:11; Jer. 6:3; 23:1–4; Ezek. 34:2 ff.; Micah 5:5; Nahum 3:18; Zech. 10:2 f.; 11:3–6; etc.

22. Acts 3:12–26: rather than "Son of God," Jesus is called "the Christ"; Acts 4:24–30: Jesus is the anointed of Ps. 2 and the servant; Acts 7:37, 52, 55–56, 59–60: the Mosaic tradition is set alongside that of Ps. 110 and the resurrection.

23. Luke places the giving of these commandments in a sermon on the plain (Luke 6:17, 20–49).

24. The Synoptic parallels are interesting here. Mark 9:3 refers only to the glistening whiteness of Jesus' garments; Luke 9:29 adds that Jesus' countenance was altered; Matthew alone says his face shone. Cf. John 1:14; II Cor. 3:7 to 4:6.

25. 1 Q S 9:10 f.; 4 Q Test. 5–8.

26. A different and fragmentary tradition makes Moses' own sin the reason for Yahweh's refusal to allow Moses to enter the Promised Land (Num. 20:12; 27:12–14; Deut. 32:51).

27. Von Rad, *Old Testament Theology,* Vol. II, pp. 261–262.

28. See Fuller, *op. cit.,* p. 153.

29. Rev. 1:16; 2:12, 16, describe the Son of Man in terms of Isa. 49:2, which is part of the second Servant Song, Isa. 49:1–6.

30. So Fuller, *op. cit.*, p. 153.

31. Ex. 6:6; 15:13; Deut. 7:8; 9:26; 13:5; 15:15; 21:8; 24:18; II Sam. 7:23; Neh. 1:10; Micah 6:4; Ps. 78:35; Isa. 63:9.

32. Isa. 41:14; 43:14; 44:6, 24; 47:4; 48:17; 49:7, 26; 54:5, 8; cf. ch. 63:16.

33. Isa. 43:1; 44:22 f.; 48:20; 52:9.

34. See H. H. Guthrie, *Israel's Sacred Songs* (The Seabury Press, Inc., 1966), Ch. 2.

35. Fuller, *op. cit.*, pp. 152–153. Fuller supports his view by saying that the references to the fulfillment of Scripture in the Son of Man sayings of Mark 8:31; 9:12; and 14:21 have Ps. 118:22 in mind, but this is conjecture.

36. Ex. 4:22; Jer. 31:20; Isa. 63:16; 64:8; Deut. 8:5; 32:18; cf. Rom. 9:4.

37. The Son is preexistent also in Rom. 8:3; Gal. 4:4; Col. 1:13–17; Heb. 1:2; I John 4:9; etc.

38. It is this theme of light and darkness, drawn from the Old Testament and used repeatedly by John, which most convincingly points to the Old Testament as the background of John, ch. 1, contra Fuller, *op. cit.*, pp. 222–227, who derives John, ch. 1, from the *sophia-logos* myth in Hellenistic Judaism. See my article "Jesus Christ, the Light of the World: The Biblical Understanding of Light and Darkness," *Interpretation,* Oct. 1963, pp. 439–449.

39.
Matt. 1:22 f.	: Isa.	7:14
Matt. 2:5–6	: Micah	5:2
Matt. 2:14–15	: Hos.	11:1
Matt. 2:17–18	: Jer.	31:15
Matt. 4:14–16	: Isa.	9:1–2
Matt. 8:17	: Isa.	53:4
Matt. 12:17–21	: Isa.	42:1–4
Matt. 13:14–15	: Isa.	6:9–10
Matt. 13:35	: Ps.	78:2
Matt. 21:4–5	: Zech.	9:9
Matt. 27:9	: Zech.	11:12–13

40. This identification of Jesus' death with baptism is suggested also in Mark 10:38–39 and par. and Luke 12:50.

41. This is the meaning of Ex. 19:6, in which Israel is to be

"a holy nation." Sainthood or holiness in the Bible does not refer in most instances to moral perfection. Rather, its connotation is that of being separated out, of being reserved for the purpose of God. Thus Paul addresses the quarreling, divided, immoral Corinthians as "saints," "*hagioi*," "holy ones" (I Cor. 1:2; II Cor. 1:1), a title he often uses in addressing his churches (Rom. 1:7; Phil. 1:1).

42. Although the Rechabites and Nazirites in the Old Testament both withdrew into closed colonies, following their own customs, as protests against the surrounding culture, a trend continued then in communities such as Qumran and the monastic movements.

43. Cf. John 20:22; I John 3:24; Mark 1:8.

44. The prophets all have oracles addressed to the foreign nations, but there is no evidence that these oracles were delivered outside Israel.

Chapter VI. REMOVING THE OBSTACLES TO THE
WORD OF THE LORD

1. A comparative examination of the lessons most recently selected by denominations using a three-year cycle of pericopes—the Episcopal Church, the Lutheran Church in America, the Roman Catholic Church, The United Presbyterian Church U.S.A., and the United Church of Christ—reveals that there is agreement on about 75 percent of the lessons. The major divergencies appear in the Presbyterian *Worshipbook*, whose lectionary has been adopted by the United Church of Christ. The differences are particularly great during Lent and Holy Week. In addition, the Episcopalians and the Roman Catholics list responsive psalms for each day.

2. One suspects that this is the reason for the recommendation of four long lessons from Proverbs on the third to sixth Sundays after Epiphany in *The Book of Common Worship*, 1946, The United Presbyterian Church U.S.A.

3. For example, why should Isa. 11:1–9 have v. 10 added to it (in *The Book of Worship*, 1964, second Sunday in Advent), or on what basis can v. 8 properly be left off of Eccl. 12:1–7 (*Service Book and Hymnal*, 1958, Lutheran Church in America, first Sunday after Epiphany)?

4. *The Book of Common Prayer*, 1944, Episcopal Church.

5. *The Book of Common Worship*, 1946.

6. *Services of the Church* (United Church Press, 1969), No. 7, p. 1.

7. Each of the passages listed contains many other possible sermon texts besides the one quoted, and always the passage must be dealt with as a unit.

8. Verses 7–9 very much belong to the "lostness" of Israel in Ps. 137.

9. The invitation of Jesus in Matt. 11:28–30 is framed in words similar to the invitation of Wisdom in Ecclus. 51:23–26.

10. For other references to the yoke of men, see Isa. 9:4; 10: 24–27; 47:6; 58:6–9; Jer., chs. 27 and 28; 30:8–9; Ezek. 34:27; Lev. 26:13; I Kings 12:1–15; Acts 15:10; Phil. 4:3.

11. The story of Gen., ch. 3, is of course symbolic of the way mankind as a whole has acted in relation to God. *'adam* is the Hebrew term for mankind.

12. For example, the lectionary of the United Church of Christ.

13. For example, the Reference Edition of the RSV (Thomas Nelson & Sons, Inc., 1959).

14. Sermon on Isa. 60:1 heard in St. Peter's United Church of Christ, Lancaster, Pa., Dec. 3, 1972.

15. Unless otherwise stated, the examples used in the following discussions in this chapter are outlines of sermons presented by working pastors in my graduate seminar on Old Testament Hermeneutics at Lancaster Theological Seminary. Their authors are best left nameless.

16. "Moral Choice in a Bountiful Land," Dwight E. Stevenson, *Pulpit*, Jan., 1968, pp. 19–21.

17. H. H. Rowley, *The Re-discovery of the Old Testament* (The Westminster Press, 1946), pp. 174 ff.

18. C. S. Lewis, *Reflections on the Psalms* (London: Geoffrey Bles, Ltd., 1958).

19. T. H. Robinson, *Poetry and Poets of the Old Testament* (London: Gerald Duckworth & Co., Ltd., 1947), p. 122.

20. Walter Russell Bowie, in *The Interpreter's Bible* (Abingdon-Cokesbury Press, 1952), Vol. I, p. 754.

21. Albert George Butzer, in *The Interpreter's Bible*, Vol. II, pp. 148–152.

22. Elizabeth Achtemeier, "Hosea—Prophet of the Heart," *Bible Studies* (Board of Parish Education, Lutheran Church in America, 1972).

23. Terence Y. Mullins, editor, *ibid.*, p. 42.

Chapter VII. VALID METHOD AND SOME SAMPLE SERMONS

1. Mary Jean Irion, "The Cliché That Is Christmas," *United Church Herald,* Dec., 1967, p. 29.

2. This sermon was published in a somewhat different form, as a reflection about the ministry, in the now defunct *Theology and Life,* Fall, 1966, pp. 199 ff.

Index of Scriptural References

In some cases a number of short passages have been indexed together under an inclusive reference. To find mention of a specific verse or passage, refer to all the pages listed in an entry.

217

220

221

223